1 MONTH OF
FREE
READING

at

www.ForgottenBooks.com

By purchasing this book you are eligible for one month membership to ForgottenBooks.com, giving you unlimited access to our entire collection of over 1,000,000 titles via our web site and mobile apps.

To claim your free month visit:

www.forgottenbooks.com/free893085

ISBN 978-0-265-81132-0
PIBN 10893085

W.F.Bohlender   Peter Bohlender   Harry N.Kyle

SALUTATION

To the thousands of our friends and customers, whom it has been our privilege and pleasure to serve in the past, and to the many thousands whom we hope to serve in the future, we send a cordial greeting:

We desire to extend to our many satisfied friends and customers our sincere thanks for their patronage, and the assurance that we are better prepared than ever before to supply their wants.. To those who have never dealt with us, but whom we should like to include among our friends, we shall be glad to demonstrate the high quality of our stock, our ability to handle all orders and our high class methods of doing business.

Through all the years of the firm's business existence down to the present, it has always been the sincere aim, and the unswerving purpose of the men who compose this firm to live up to such a high mark of square dealing and business integrity that they could command the respect, and justly merit the confidence of their fellowmen, and we are happy to say to our many loyal friends and customers, that this policy has proved a success. That our patrons are our friends is made evident to us in many valued letters received expressing approval of the quality of stock sent, careful packing and general satisfactory manner of handling the business which has been entrusted to us.

In many ways we have been favored, and with a sense of sincere appreciation, we enter upon a new year of business, better equipped than ever before for handling our steadily growing trade.

Now at the beginning of another year, we come to you with our offering of the best varieties of Fruit and Ornamental Trees, Small Fruits, Shrubs, Evergreens, Perennials, etc., and take pride in the knowledge that what we have to offer is absolutely the best.

Peter Bohlender & Sons
SPRING HILL NURSERIES, TIPPECANOE CITY, OHIO

SPRING HILL NURSERIES

TIPPECANOE CITY, (MIAMI COUNTY) OHIO.

DATE.. 19......

NAME ....

P. O. ....

COUNTY........................... STATE...............

STREET........................... R. F. D...............

SHIPPING POINT ....

COUNTY ....

FREIGHT......................... EXPRESS............

Please Do Not Write Here

U. S. De........

Check—Money Order—Express Order—Draft—Currency—Amount Enclosed $

While we exercise the greatest care to have all trees, shrubs and plants sold by us true to name and free from disease, and hold ourselves prepared to replace, on proper proof, all that may prove to be otherwise, we do not give any warranty, expressed or implied, with respect to them, and all such goods are sold upon the express condition and understanding that in case any of them prove to be untrue to name, unhealthy or otherwise defective, we shall not be held responsible for a greater amount than the original price of the goods.

NUMBER	ARTICLES WANTED	Price Each	Dollars Cts.
		Amount Enclosed $	

ORDER BLANK—Continued

NUMBER	ARTICLES WANTED	Price Each	Dollars	Cts.
		Amount Enclosed $		

Below are the addresses of friends interested in fruit and ornamental trees. Please send them your catalog on "Trees That Grow."

Express Prepaid On All Orders of $4.00 or More.

MR. J. B. CROUCH

We are pleased to introduce to you J. B. Crouch, who is now associated with us as manager of our Mail Order Department. It will be his pleasure to answer all correspondence, give information concerning nursery stock and direct the filling and shipping of all orders.

Mr. Crouch has had a life time experience in supplying the needs of human life in many ways and will give you service that it is impossible for you to obtain elsewhere.

You will never regret meeting him either socially or in a business way and becoming better acquainted with him. This is a guarantee that any Bank, Business Firm or Resident of our local community will give him.

QUALITY OF STOCK

The stock that we offer and deliver to our customers in this catalog is the very best that is possible to produce. The fact is, the cream of the nursery.

Some salesmen claim that stock sold through catalogs is of an inferior quality. This is not true with the Peter Bohlender & Sons, as the stock that we offer is of the highest quality, and we ship nothing but the best. And with our standing as nurserymen, this is a guarantee that is worth something to you.

Our Guarantee. Specifies that all stock will be exactly as represented as to size, name, and general specifications. It is good, clean, healthy, and first-class. If at any time found otherwise, we will replace same free of charge or refund the money paid for same.

Our Watchword. Good stock, well dug, carefully selected and promptly shipped; modern methods, square dealing, and a guarantee that you receive fullest possible value for your money—this is our watchword.

Order by Mail. When you order from us by mail, you do not take any undue risk. There is no chance for misunderstanding. We would not make these promises and send them through the mails if we did not live up to them. All State and Government experimental stations recommend buying direct from nursery. We carry nothing but well-tried varieties. The Certificate of Inspection and our liberal guarantee are both full protection to you.

Small Orders. We appreciate all orders, and small ones receive as careful attention and will be shipped as promptly as large ones.

Large Orders. If large orders are to be placed, it is especially advised to send in the list of stock at just as early a date as possible, so that stock may be reserved for the order.

Order Early. It is always best to order early. NOW, when you receive this catalog, is just the right time of the year. The demand for our stock is invariably larger than the supply, because we burn thousands of plants every season to keep the general quality of our merchandise up to its highest point.

Packing. Packing is done in boxes or paper-lined bales, and plenty of damp packing material is used. No charge is made for boxes or packing, nor for delivery to your freight or express depots.

Remittance. Should accompany the order. It saves time, overhead expenses, chances for errors, and insurers quicker service. You can make your remittance in any way most convenient for you. However, we are always ready to extend credit to any one deserving it.

Transportation. We pay all transportation charges on all orders amounting to $4.00 or more, and the stock is guaranteed to arrive at your express office in good condition. If any of this stock should be damaged in transit, write us immediately and we will either replace the stock free of charge or refund the money paid for same.

Errors. We exercise the utmost care in filling all orders, striving to do a little more than we offer; nevertheless, in the press of the season, errors will sometimes occur, in which case we ask to be promptly notified of the fact, and will make such correction as will be satisfactory. Please keep a copy of order for comparison.

Correspondence Solicited. We gladly answer all inquiries promptly and to the best of our ability. For the use of our patrons and friends, we have installed a special department where all questions are answered direct. If any information relative to horticultural pursuits is desired, we are at all times ready and willing to furnish same.

Location. Our nursery is located on the B. & O. Railroad and on the Dayton & Troy interurban line. Our office and packing grounds are one square south of the Dayton & Troy car barns and five squares south of the B. & O. railroad station.

Shipping Facilities. We can either ship by Parcels Post, Freight or Express. The B.

& O. sidetrack is within a few feet of our packing sheds, and is our nursery switch. The Dayton & Troy Traction freight station is within a square of our packing grounds, and we have a private switch within a few feet of our sheds. The American Railway Express Co. is also convenient. All stock is delivered on board cars at Tippecanoe City, Miami County, Ohio, at the prices quoted in this book, except where otherwise noted. We make no charges for packing.

Pointers for Planters

Success with trees and plants depends, in a large measure, upon the treatment given them when first received.

Remove from the express or freight office as soon as possible.

Be sure to avoid all unnecessary exposure to the air and sun.

If possible, plant as soon as received. When this cannot be done, it is best to heel in. Select a well-drained, shaded spot. Dig a trench deep enough to accommodate the roots. Unpack the box or bale, shake all packing material from the roots and place the trees in trench, inclined at an angle of forty-five degrees or more, cover to a depth of ten to twelve inches, and water thoroughly. Finish by throwing on more soil until all roots are covered. Care should be taken to fill the spaces between the roots. Too much care cannot be given to this, as each root that is not in contact with the soil is bound to die.

Preparing the Soil

The preparation of the soil is the first important requisite to the successful raising of an orchard. This should be made dry and rich. Underdrained, if necessary, as trees will not thrive in soil constantly saturated with stagnant water.

If at all feasible, plow up the whole area to be planted, if possible, with a sub-soil plow and get the whole area in good farming condition.

Preparing the Trees for Planting

Cut off the ends of all broken or bruised roots with a sharp knife, making a clean cut. This pruning of the roots should be followed by a pruning of the top. Decide when the trees are planted, the height at which the top or head is to start. Think first of the best possible shape and size. For most practical purposes and for most trees, a low, open head is desirable, as it is the easiest to work over and to pick the fruit from.

Planting

When all is in readiness for planting, dig the holes at least three feet square and eighteen inches deep.

Place the tree in the center and fill in the soil that was taken from the top first, and firm it well around the roots. If the ground is at all dry, give a goodly supply of water. After this has settled away, fill in the remainder of the dirt and firm well again. Do not allow any manure to come in contact with the roots, but a good coating on top as a mulch will be beneficial. Always plant the trees from one to two inches deeper than in the nursery row.

CERTIFICATE OF INSPECTION IS ATTACHED TO EACH SHIPMENT AND PACKAGE

Quality Apple Trees

When the hardiness, productiveness, and commercial value of the apple is considered, it is, by common consent, the "King of the Fruits." America is the great apple-producting country of the world, as practically every state in the Union and many parts of Canada produce apples. The demand is much larger than the supply, so there is no danger of over-production. Some localities are more favored than others as to soil and climate and grow the greater part of the apples for our export trade; but every ₁an_d-owner should grow enough to supply his own family with fruit the entire year.

In selecting our varieties for cultivation, it has been our constant aim to select only those of standard excellence, and in no instance do we- recommend a novelty without first ascertaining its history from a reliable source. So, from the list we offer, varieties may be selected that are adapted to any locality. If you are in doubt as to those best adapted for your planting, we will gladly give you the benefit of our wider experience and make a selection for you.

The ideal soil for apples is a strong loam of a limestone nature, but apples will thrive on almost any soil, providing it is well drained. Recent investigation has shown that a surplus of water—that is, poor drainage—will cause the fruit to be of poor quality and flavor.

Our fruit trees are either budded or grafted. We use only the varieties that give the best results and give the longest-lived trees. Seedling roots used in the propagation of apple trees, are especially grown for this purpose. The scions or wood of the varieties wanted are cut from scion orchards where the trees are always kept in healthy condition, so there is no chance of carrying new disease into other orchards.

With the new spray material, which is especially prepared at a very reasonable price, any one can grow perfect fruit with less expense and labor than ever before.

We grow trees on land that produces the best and most perfect trees, never growing the second crop of apple trees on the same piece of land. This insures you the best quality and the most vigorous and healthy trees obtainable

and it means success of your orchard for future years. You may not be able to tell the difference in the trees when you first get them, but you no doubt have seen some orchards live to 50 years or more and still be in a healthy condition, and other orchards near them existing only a few years, and even a nurseryman can not tell the difference between the trees when they are taken from the nursery rows.

When planting an orchard it is the future you must consider.

APPLE TREES Guaranteed First Class

	Each	10	25	100
2-yr., 2-3 ft...	$	$3.00	$ 6.75	$24.00
2-yr., 3-4 ft...	.50	4.50	10.00	35.00
2-yr., 4-5 ft...	.75	7.00	16.25	60.00
2-yr., 5-7 ft...	1.00	9.00	21.25	80.00

Remember we prepay express or freight charges on all orders of $4.00 or more.

Plant Apple Trees 30 feet apart, either Spring or late Fall. Trees that grow and produce what you buy are the cheapest after all. This is the reason why we have customers who have patronized us almost 50 years.

Summer Apples

EARLY HARVEST (Early June, Yellow Harvest)— The Early Harvest has been in cultivation for more than one hundred years. It is a desirable variety for the home orchard because of its earliness and excellency for dessert and culinary purposes. Fruit is medium size to large; the skin tender, very smooth, clear pale waxen yellow; flesh is white, rather fine, crisp, tender, juicy, at first briskly subacid, but eventually becoming milder and more agreeable for dessert. Ripens in July and August.

RED ASTRACHAN—A very beautiful, early summer apple of good medium size; yellow, largely covered with red, presenting a striped appearance; flesh white, often strongly tinged with red, crisp, tender, juicy, subacid, good to very good. One of the most beautiful early market apples. Tree is medium size, a good grower, extra hardy, moderately long lived; comes into bearing rather young and is a reliable cropper, yielding moderate to good crops biennially, or sometimes yearly. Can be grown anywhere in the United States. Ripens in August.

YELLOW TRANSPARENT (White Transparent, Grand Sultan)—Another well known and popular Russian variety that should be in every orchard. The tree is a very upright grower and usually bears fruit the first year after planting, often in the nursery rows. Fruit of medium size, pale waxen yellow, pleasantly acid, tender and good, splendid for home and for market. Ripens in July and August, before Early Harvest.

Buying Spring Hill Nursery stock is an investment in absolute satisfaction. You are sure of receiving the stock ordered in the best possible condition. Shipments are made at the time specified. All plants are true to name. It is our aim to give our friends and customers just a little better values than our catalog offers, all the time.

EARLY HARVEST

Fall Varieties

DUCHESS OF OLDENBURG, or **DUCHESS**—A Russian variety of great hardiness, yielding abundantly in all sections. Fruits are large, rounded, yellow, striped/red, tender, juicy and of the best quality for cooking.

FALL BAMBO—A pretty, mottled and striped red and yellow apple, of medium size and good flavor; widely cultivated and highly esteemed for eating. The tree is a strong grower and heavy bearer. October to December.

FALLAWATER, or **TULPEHOCKEN**—Large and handsome, green, nearly covered with dull red. Bears young and abundantly. January to April.

MAIDEN BLUSH—One of the most beautiful and most productive fall varieties. A good market sort, because of the attractiveness of the fruit. Of uniformly good size, smooth, round, beautifully flushed with brilliant red on a yellow ground. Good for table use. August and September.

WEALTHY—This apple originated in Minnesota and is notable for its hardiness of tree and fruit bud. Large, smooth, almost overspread with bright red. Very attractive. Absolutely the best apple of its season. It is a good keeper, splendid for cold storage. October and January.

Winter Varieties

ARKANSAS BLACK—A remarkable, large, and handsome crimson-black apple; perfectly smooth, roundish flat, lightly dotted with white. The flesh is yellow and delicious; an excellent keeper. It is popular in the South where it commands double the price of the Ben Davis. December to April.

BALDWIN—Probably no apple has secured so general popularity. When grown on trees well open to the sun, it is a bright red and very rich. Is a great market apple, very productive; large, deep red, crisp, juicy flesh. December to March.

BANANA—Tree a good grower; bears very young and annually; hardy. The fruit is large, clear, pale yellow with pinkish red blush; the flesh is tender and aromatic. It has a suggestion of the banana flavor. Recommended for fancy market, but will stand long shipment. Excellent for dessert. November to February.

BEN DAVIS (New York Pippin—Thornton of Southern Alabama)—A remarkable keeper and profitable market apple in many sections. Large hand-

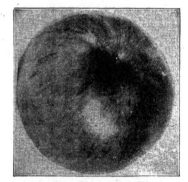

DUCHESS OF OLDENBURG

MAIDEN BLUSH

some, brightly striped with red, variable in flavor. Remarkably vigorous and fruitful. January to April.

DELICIOUS—These trees come into bearing early and produce heavy annual crops. The fruit is extra large, brilliant dark red shaded to yellow at blossom end. Flesh white and tender. Rich flavor, slightly subacid.

FAMEUSE (Snow Apple)—An old and well known variety that usually sells above the average market price and keeps well until the holidays. Tree a vigorous grower, hardy, and bears enormous crops of medium size fruit, that is smooth and regular; deep crimson, with snowy white flesh of delightful flavor. November to January.

GANO—Similar, but superior to Ben Davis, bearing a much handsomer and better quality of fruit, that is large and dark red. The pale yellow flesh is mild subacid, of good flavor and good keeping qualities. It is a profitable market variety. December to February.

GRIMES GOLDEN—A medium to large apple of transparent golden yellow; very best quality. Flesh tender, juicy, spicy and rich. An old-time favorite that has never lost its popularity. The hardy, vigorous tree produces large crops, blooms late, and comes into bearing young. Largely planted in the South and Southwest. A favorite in all markets and invariably brings highest price. November to February.

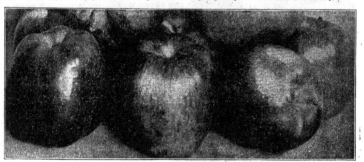

DELICIOUS APPLES

ROME BEAUTY

HUBBARDSTON NONSUCH (American Blush)—The tree is a very handsome, strong grower, and bears heavy crops. A very large, handsome apple, yellow overlaid with red; tender flesh, with distinct, delightful flavor. November to January.

JONATHAN—This is recognized as the most popular apple, in the West. If put into cold storage promptly after being picked, the Jonathan keeps better than nearly any apple grown. It is medium sized, pale yellow, heavily flushed with red; the flesh is white, juicy, tender and mild subacid. Excellent quality. November to March.

KING OF TOMPKINS COUNTY—A red apple of extraordinary size and fair quality; the flesh is slightly coarse, but tender. An abundant bearer. November to March.

MAMMOTH BLACK TWIG—A very showy, dark red winter apple of good quality. Tree is a strong, vigorous grower, hardy, and a regular and abundant bearer. Largely planted in Arkansas as superior to Winesap. November to April.

McINTOSH RED—Tree a vigorous grower, forming a roundish spreading head. Fruit is from medium to large, uniform size and shape. Flesh slightly tinged with yellow, sometimes veined with red; crisp, juicy, subacid, becoming mild, almost sweet, when ripe. Splendid for dessert. October to December.

NORTHWESTERN GREENING—This is an annual, abundant-bearing sort. The tree and fruit buds are very hardy. The fruit is large, greenish yellow when ripe; good flavor, juicy and subacid. Good keeper. January to June.

NORTHERN SPY—Large, striped crimson in the sun, juicy, rich, and aromatic, retaining these qualities until late spring or summer. The tree grows rapidly, bears well as it blooms later than most varieties. Valuable as an aphis-resisting sort. This apple has taken its place quite at the front of winter varieties over a very large territory. January to June.

PEWAUKEE—Medium to large, round, oblate, bright yellow, flushed with dull red; has white, tender flesh of good quality. Tree is exceptionally hardy and robust, well suited to cold climates.

ROME BEAUTY (Royal Red, Roma, Phoenix)—These trees come into bearing early and produce heavy annual crops of fruit, uniform in size, fine in appearance, and of good quality. The fruit is large and handsome, yellow with crimson cheek, tender, juicy, yellow flesh. November to February.

SPITZENBERG—Large, brilliant red with gray dots; rich, crisp, juicy and delicious. Tree rather a slow grower, but with good cultivation forms a large, spreading tree. Good bearer. December to April.

STARK—Large, roundish, golden-green with crimson shadings; flesh yellow, moderately juicy, mild subacid. The tree makes a strong growth, bears early and abundantly regular crops. One of the best apples. January to May.

STAYMAN'S WINESAP—One of the finest apples grown for appearance, flavor, and juiciness. A favorite for cider. Medium size, mostly covered with red on a yellow ground; flesh fine, crisp, juicy, very tender, and highly flavored. The tree is a strong grower, a drought resister, and will thrive on thin soil. No apple is more widely planted. November to April, but will keep until May.

TOLMAN'S SWEET—Tree a free grower. Fruit medium size, yellow, firm and sweet. December to April.

WAGNER—A fine, deep red apple of medium size to large; flesh firm, subacid, and well flavored, of excellent quality, somewhat resembles the Northern Spy. The tree is an upright grower and productive, but usually is short-lived. The tree bears when young and yields good annual crops that are good from December to May.

WHITE PIPPIN—One of our cleanest and largest winter apples of fine quality. The tree is a good bearer and long lived. The fruit is creamy yellow with tender white flesh of pleasantly acid taste. January to June.

STAYMAN'S WINESAP

WINESAP—One of the very best keepers, popular with fruit stores because it always holds up, and one of the leading export apples. Fruit medium large, skin almost entirely covered with dark red, flesh yellow, crisp, with a rich flavor. This is a standard well known and productive variety of the West and Southwest. December to March.

YORK IMPERIAL (Johnson's Fine Winter, Shepp, etc.)—This tree is vigorous and long lived. Bears annual crops of medium-sized, attractive, smooth, clear, waxen-yellow fruit, flushed with carmine. The flesh is crisp, firm, subacid, a good keeper and retains its flavor to the last. December to February.

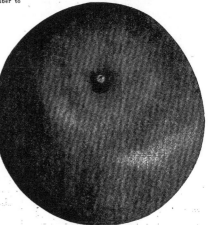

KING OF TOMPKINS COUNTY

Crab Apples

Crab apples are especially desirable in the colder sections as only a few varieties of apples can be successfully grown; but they succeed well in all climates and their fruit is very popular for preserves, jelly and some sorts are excellent for eating. The Crab Apples do well on almost all soils. Come into bearing early and bear almost every year.

TRANSCENDENT—This is the largest and best of the Siberian Crabs. The tree is extremely hardy, good grower, and usually very productive. The fruits are about one and a half to two inches in diameter. Bright yellow striped with red, flesh crisp, juicy and subacid. August to September.

WHITNEY—The tree is a hardy, thrifty, upright grower, and comes into bearing when young; it is a very productive variety. The flesh is yellowish, crisp, juicy and splendid for eating and cider. August and September.

The stock we sell is cared for from the time the seed or plant is planted until it is packed and shipped on your order. There is no labor too great for us to undertake to maintain the reputation we have built up in the more than sixty years of our business life.

Mr. J. Frank Robb, New Philadelphia, Ohio, writes: "It is a rare occasion that I take the time to write and inform anyone that I am more than pleased with their goods or products, but I have a reason to tell you that your plants and the rose I purchased from you a short time ago superior to any that I have ever purchased that there is no comparison whatever."

TRANSPARENT CRAB

COLLECTION NO. 10

Apple, Pear, Plum, Cherry and Quince Trees. Our regular price on this list, $20.95. Our price to you, express prepaid to your express office **$12.25**

2 Stayman's Winesap Apple—Fine quality, best winter.
1 Northern Spy Apple—Good winter.
1 Rambo—You know this one.
2 Delicious Apple—Fine dessert; winter.
1 Red Astrachan Apple—Early red.
1 Yellow Transparent Apple—Early.
1 Bartlett Pear—Best Canning pear.
1 Duchess Pear—Fine fall pear.

1 Keiffer Pear—Fine; winter.
1 Lombard Plum—Seldom fails to bear fruit.
1 Bradshaw Plum—Large blue; fine quality
1 Montmorency Cherry—Sour; fine; late.
1 Early Richmond Cherry—Sour; dark red.
1 Orange Quince—Best variety.
2 Champion Peach—White, red cheeked.
2 Elberta Peach—Yellow freestone.

These trees are the highest quality, best grade and guaranteed to arrive in good condition. You are taking no chances, as you can not buy better trees if you pay double the price.

George Henderson, Bellefontaine, Ohio, writes: Enclosed find the balance on the plants. They were received in very good condition. Thanks for your prompt attention to our order.

Buying poor trees just because you can buy them cheap, is poor economy. You would not do this in buying your hogs, cattle, or chickens; why do it with trees? There is usually something wrong when goods are sold below the market price, but the buyer usually pays the bill.

Pears, the Quality Fruit

Our Pear trees are of the finest quality for transplanting, for they are well-developed, stocky trees. In the course of five years they will be bearing a fine crop of fruit. We have both standard and dwarf varieties. For the permanent orchard we recommend the standard varieties, the dwarf being better for a small lot.

BARTLETT PEAR

A strong loam of moderate depth, or a dry subsoil, is best adapted to the pears, but they will adapt themselves to as great a variety of soil as any other fruit. The soil should not be too rich, as a rapid growth is more likely to produce blight. The dwarf trees should be pruned every year. Thin the fruit whenever the trees are heavily burdened, particularly the young trees.

PEAR TREES, GUARANTEED TO BE FIRST-CLASS, 2 AND 3 YEARS OLD

	Each	10	25
Standard Pear Trees, 3-4 ft..	$ .60	$5.00	$12.00
Standard Pear Trees, 4-5 ft..	.75	7.00	16.25
Standard Pear Trees, 5-7 ft..	1.25	10.00	24.00

Plant in Spring and late Fall, 20 feet apart. Remember all stock we offer is of the highest quality, grown by the best and most skilled labor, and in soil conditions that make them grow, and we prepay express charges on your order.

ANJOU (Buerre d'Anjou)—Rather large; flesh yellowish-white; fine grained, melting, with a rich, excellent flavor. Has good keeping qualities.

BARTLETT—One of the most popular sorts, both for home and market. It is large, handsome waxen yellow, with red blush; flesh buttery, rich and juicy, highly flavored. One of the best varieties for canning. Ripens in August and September.

CLAPP'S FAVORITE—Fruit handsome, large, long, yellow, spotted dull red where exposed to the sun; flesh fine grained, juicy, rich, sweet flavored. It resembles the Bartlett. The tree is a vigorous grower, hardy and productive. Ripens in August.

DUCHESS D'ANGOULEME—This is the largest among our really good pears. The skin is a dull greenish yellow; flesh white, melting, juicy and well flavored. The tree is a vigorous grower and a reliable bearer. A profitable market variety and fair for home use. October and November.

FLEMISH BEAUTY—One of the best varieties of pears for the Southwest, on account of its hardiness. The tree is a strong grower, an annual and abundant bearer, and is usually successful over a large range of country. The fruit is large; the skin pale yellow; the flavor is sweet and melting. September and October.

KIEFFER—On account of the excellent keeping qualities it is one of the best and most profitable market varieties. Fine for canning or preserving. For commercial orchard it is undoubtedly one of the best. The trees are not troubled with scale, and seldom fail to bear a good crop. Trees bear young. October and November.

KOONCE—An exceedingly hardy variety, in fact almost frost-proof, as it will bear heavy crops when all other varieties are destroyed by frost. A handsome pear of medium size. July and August.

SECKLE—This well known little pear has attained the rank of standard in quality on account of its rich delicious flavor; very popular for dessert. August and September.

SHELDON—A pear of the finest quality, rich and highly aromatic. The fruit is greenish russet with a red cheek; large size and somewhat flattened shape. Sept.

KIEFFER PEAR

WHITE STAR—Provides fruit all the year. This pear is un-equalled for keeping qualities, extremely hardy, unusually productive, and a great commercial pear. The fruit has been known to keep until May and June of the following year, just under ordinary care in a common cellar. This pear has the size of the Barlett. Good for dessert.

WHITE STAR

We can furnish you a number of affidavits as to its keeping qualities and productiveness. This variety is seldom known to have a crop failure. In fact, the history of the original shows that it never has missed a crop after it commenced bearing. The tree has borne as much as thirty bushels of fruit and practically every pear perfect. $1.00 each; 3 for $2.50.

Dwarf Fruits

The dwarf fruits are not nearly so common or well known as they are in Europe or as they should be here. The fruits are just the same as on the standard varieties. The only difference is, the trees or plants do not take so much room as many of them may be trained on the fence, an espalier or even along the side of a building if necessary. They also come into bearing much earlier than the standard sorts. It is possible to plant three to five hundred dwarf trees on a quarter of an acre of ground, where less than a dozen standard varieties would flourish. The dwarf fruit trees also work more readily into a scheme of more or less ornamental gardening, where fruits are combined with flowers, especially if some sort of formal gardening is attempted. The cordon, espalier, and pyramids exactly suit these demands.

Dwarf Apples

Dwarf Apples are produced by grafting the variety desired onto the dwarf paraside stock, raised for this purpose. Plant one year old trees. They will develop into any shaped tree you wish to train them and will produce fruit in a very few years. In fact, one-year-old trees often produce fruit in the nursery rows the second year.

DWARF APPLE TREES—1 year old, 2 to 3 feet, 50c each; $4.00 per 10. 3 to 4 feet, 60c each; $5.00 per 10.

VARIETIES—Jonathan, McIntosh, Early Harvest, Stark, Transparent, Banana. Plant in spring or late fall, 6 to 8 feet apart.

Dwarf Pears

The Pear is very profitably grown as a "dwarf." These pears differ from the stand-ards inasmuch as they are propagated on a quince root, which makes it slow growing and dwarfish. The fruit is the same in either case. The quality and appearance of the fruit will convince any one that they are excellent to plant.

DWARF PEARS—Select trees, 2 and 3 years old, 3 to 4 feet, 75c each; $7.00 per 10; $16.25 per 25.
VARIETIES—Duchess, Bartlett, Kieffer, Flemish Beauty, Clapp's Favorite, Seckle.
Plant Spring and Fall, 8 to 10 feet apart.

In comparing prices remember we prepay all transportation charges on orders of $4.00 or more.

Collection No. 23

How you can save some money. 10 Pears, 4 feet and up. First class trees, $5.50.
- 3 Bartlett
- 2 Flemish Beauty
- 2 Duchess Dwarf
- 1 Sheldon
- 1 Keiffer
- 1 Anjou (Buerre d'Anjou)

The above selection of Pear Trees will give you fruit from August to February. The best quality of Pears.

Collection No. 22

Special offer on Dwarf Fruits. 12 Trees for $8.75. Following Kinds:
This is an excellent selection and a real bargain.
- 3 Duchess Pear, 3 to 4 feet.
- 1 Bartlett Pear, 3 to 4 feet.
- 1 Keiffer Pear, 3 to 4 feet.
- 1 Flemish Pear, 3 to 4 feet.
- 1 Clapp Favorite, 3 to 4 feet.
- 1 Seckle Pear, 3 to 4 feet.
- 1 Jonathan Apple, 2 to 3 feet.
- 1 Red McIntosh Apple, 3 to 4 feet.
- 1 Banana Apple, 3 to 4 feet.
- 1 Stark Apple, 3 to 4 feet.

CROSBY PEACHES

Thrifty Peach Trees

If living on a farm, plant a small peach orchard for home use or a larger one for commercial purposes. If living on a city lot, plant a peach tree in the back yard. This tree, if cared for, will produce enough fruit for a small family. No difference whether one tree is planted or many, they are sure to pay large dividends. In spite of the fact that large peach orchards are planted each year, still there are never enough to supply the market.

A deep, rich, sandy loam, that is well drained, is best suited to peach trees. Before transplanting the trees, be sure to trim off every branch close to the tree, and cut back the stem of the tree itself about one-third. To have a perfectly formed, round-headed tree, they should be trimmed each year.

Our peach trees are all propagated from peach seeds secured from North Carolina, where there are no peach "yellows," or any other fatal diseases. All of our varieties are budded on this high-class stcok. They are fine, thrifty, well-rooted trees that will give good results.

PRICES OF PEACH TREES

	Each	10	25	100
Peach Trees, first class, 2 to 3 feet, ...$		$3.00	$ 6.50	$25.00
Peach Trees, first class, 3 to 4 feet....................	.60	5.50	12.50	45.00
Peach Trees, first class, 4 to 6 feet.................	.75	7.00	16.50	60.00

Freight and express charges prepaid on orders of $4.00 or more, east of the Mississippi River. Plant in Spring or late Fall, 16 to 18 feet apart.

BELLE OF GEORGIA—A great market peach of the South. Large, freestone peach with red cheek, red through the fine, white flesh to the seed. Firm, juicy, and excellent flavor. July.

CARMEN—A fine market variety, being the first real freestone of the season. Large, yellowish white; flesh creamy white, tender, rich and juicy. The tree is hardy, a good grower, and bears large crops regularly. A fine shipper. August.

PLANTING FRUIT IS AN INVESTMENT

No matter what the size of your property may be, fruit trees, whether few or many, are an investment. For the small place, one or two trees of several fruits will produce enough to supply the home with preserved fruit, jellies, and jams for a family of the average size for the entire winter. It will also give an abundance of fresh fruit in season, fruit that has ripened naturally and, because of its being grown on the home place, will have a flavor that no bought fruit will have.

There is no better investment on the farm than an orchard of reliable fruit trees. It does not mean an investment of a large sum of money, as it is possible to put in a certain number of trees each year until the orchard has reached the desired size. An orchard requires some attention but it always repays the care you give it in increased profits from the sale of the fruit.

Spring Hill Nursery stock is unconditionally guaranteed to be the best procurable anywhere. Our sixty years in business is in itself a guarantee that we always give satisfaction on every order placed with us.

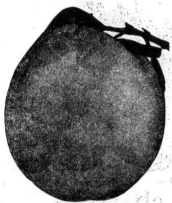

KALAMAZOO

CHAMPION—One of the finest freestone peaches. Large, creamy-white and slight blush. Flesh white, rich, sweet, juicy, and of excellent flavor. The tree is hardy and very productive. A profitable market variety, being an excellent seller and good shipper. August.

CRAWFORD'S LATE—This peach is similar to Crawford's Early, but ripens two or three weeks later.

CRAWFORD'S EARLY—A very large, rich, yellow freestone of the finest quality. Trees are very productive. This variety is perhaps better known than other varieties in the United States. Late August.

CROSBY—This peach ranks among the hardiest of peaches. Medium size, bright yellow splashed with carmine; flesh yellow and of good flavor. It is inclined to overbear, but if allowed to, the fruit will be of inferior quality. Freestone. September.

ELBERTA—One of the best varieties of the commercial orchard. The fruit is large, with golden-yellow skin covered largely with crimson; flesh is yellow, good, and firm enough to ship well. The great canning peach. The tree is a vigorous grower, healthy, fairly hardy, and a regular cropper. Freestone. August and September.

ENGLE'S MAMMOTH—Late yellow, resembles the Late Crawford but is more productive. September.

FITZGERALD—Of Canadian origin, hardy both in tree and bloom. Trees are strong growers an dvery productive, beginning to bear the second year after planting. This peach has been a success in nearly all peach sections. Fruit is bright yellow, large, suffused with red; flesh a deep yellow, firm and of very high quality. Freestone. Last of August.

HEATH CLING—Fruit very large, creamy white with faint blush. Flesh pure white to stone, juicy and sweet with a good aroma. Very popular for preserving and canning. A good keeper. October.

HALE PEACH—A large, deep golden yellow peach, overlaid with bright carmine. Smooth. Flesh firm, fine grained, and a perfect freestone. Ripens a little before the Elberta.

KALAMAZOO—An excellent variety. Fruit large, golden yellow with a crimson cheek; flesh yellow to the pit; of delightful flavor. The pit is small and freestone. The trees are hardy, productive, and bear early. September.

LEMON FREE—Large fruit, light yellow, with a greenish tinge; flesh is golden yellow, tender and juicy. Excellent for canning.

LEMON CLING—A large, oblong, yellow peach, brightened with a dark red cheek; flesh firm and rich. Tree hardy and productive. Mid September.

MOUNTAIN ROSE—A large, handsome, freestone peach, yellow skin with red cheek; the flesh is white, juicy, and most excellent. August.

NEW PROLIFIC—A popular market sort, large yellow fruit with blush cheek. The flesh is firm, juicy, fine flavor, and a freestone. The tree is a strong, vigorous grower, hardy and productive. September.

SMOCK—A large, yellow peach, mottled with red, juicy freestone. It is enormously productive and a valuable variety for the market. Late September.

CHAMPION

Cherries

For commercial purposes, plant a cherry orchard, because there is perhaps no other fruit always so much in demand at such good prices. No home orchard is complete without some cherry trees.

Cherry trees are infected by fewer diseases than any other fruit tree. The sour varieties are never troubled with scale, but spraying is, of course, beneficial to the tree.

The so-called sour varieties are hardy, vigorous, and frost-resisting. They are easily grown wherever apples succeed, and are late bloomers. Few fruit trees will bear such an abundant amount of luscious fruit year after year with as little expense. The trees are beautiful as well as useful. The "sweet" cherry thrives in many States, both east and west. It is always best to plant where the tree will be protected as much as possible from the late spring frosts. The rich, sweet, luscious cherries can be shipped long distances and are very profitable in suitable localities.

LARGE MONTMORENCY

Our cherry stock is as fine as can be produced. They are all budded on imported Mahaleb stock, which makes the best and longest-lived trees.

	Each	10	25	100
Cherry Trees, First Class, 1 year old, 2½-3½ ft.......$		$6.00	$14.00	$50.00
Cherry Trees, First Class, 2 year old, 3-4 ft........	.75	7.00	17.00	65.00
Cherry Trees, First Class, 2 year old, 4-6 ft........	1.25	10.00	24.50	95.00

GOV. WOOD

BLACK TARTARIAN—A beautiful, purplish cherry of superb quality, rich and juicy. This remarkable tree makes a beautiful, erect growth. A prolific bearer. Late June and July.

BING—One of the best known and most popular dark sweet cherries. Good for home ground. June.

DYEHOUSE—Bright red, prolific bearer. The fruit is mildly subacid, excellent variety for canning, good shipper. Free and vigorous. Last of May.

EARLY RICHMOND, or MAY—Unsurpassed for cooking. The tree is a free grower and reliable producer. The fruit is medium, dark red, juicy and has an acid flavor. June.

GOVERNOR WOOD—The standard of quality among the sweet cherries. The large, light red fruit hangs well on the tree and does not rot easily. The fruit buds are hardy and the tree is a stout, healthy grower, and an abundant bearer. June.

LATE DUKE—A large, light red cherry of most excellent quality. They are between a sweet and a sour cherry. Fine for canning. The tree is a strong, upright grower.

LARGE MONTMORENCY—Several different strains come under this variety or name; all of them are good, but we consider this particular strain one of the very best of the sour cherries, and it should be largely planted in every orchard. The fruit is large, dark red, and handsome.

NAPOLEON—Late; large, yellow sweet cherry, pink blushed; beautiful and delicious.

YELLOW SPANISH—Large, handsome, sweet cherry with light red cheek, firm and delicious. Tree vigorous in growth and productive. Late June.

The best proof of the high standard of our goods, and the satisfaction they afford is that for almost fifty years we have served the same customers in the same territory, under the same name. Our best recommendation is the fact that our old customers are constantly sending new ones to us.

Quinces

Plant Spring and Fall, 10 to 12 feet apart.

The quince is always in demand, although its commercial value has changed but little for many years. Quinces are largely used in cooking, canning, and preserving, as they have a delicious flavor. Yet the increased size of the fruit and the quality repay well for all the extra work given them. The trees thrive in almost any soil, but prefer a heavy, moist clay loam.

First Class Trees

3 to 4 ft. . $ .85 each $8.00 per 10 $19.50 per 25
4 to 5 ft.   1.00 each   9.50 per 10   22.50 per 25

CHAMPION—A strong, rugged, exceedingly productive tree, which begins to bear when two years old. The fruit is large, oval, of a rich color and excellent quality. It ripens late and keeps well until January.

APPLE, or ORANGE—Large, round, bright golden yellow, cooks quite tender, and has an excellent flavor. Valuable for preserving and for market. An abundant bearer. One of the finest late variety.

RUSSIAN MULBERRY

Mulberries

On account of the beautiful, heavy foliage and compact growth of the mulberries, they are frequently classed as ornamental trees. They are very hardy and long lived; in fact one specimen of which we know is more than three hundred years old. Throughout the Western States they are frequently planted for windbreaks and hedges, and are valuable for posts.

NEW AMERICAN—Equal to the Downing in all respects and is a much hardier tree. Vigorous grower and very productive. The best variety for fruit. The berries are very large and ripen from June to middle of September. 3 to 4 feet, 75c.

RUSSIAN—A very hardy, rapid-growing tree and very productive, but the fruit is small and of little value except as food for the birds. Often planted around orchards for this purpose. The wood is valuable for posts. 5 to 6 feet, 75c.

TABLE SHOWING NUMBER OF TREES OR PLANTS TO THE ACRE

Distance	No. of Trees	Distance	No. of Trees
1 foot apart each way	43,560	13 feet apart each way	257
2 feet apart each way	10,890	14 feet apart each way	222
3 feet apart each way	4,840	15 feet apart each way	193
4 feet apart each way	2,702	16 feet apart each way	170
5 feet apart each way	1,742	17 feet apart each way	150
6 feet apart each way	1,210	18 feet apart each way	134
7 feet apart each way	888	19 feet apart each way	120
8 feet apart each way	680	20 feet apart each way	108
9 feet apart each way	537	25 feet apart each way	69
10 feet apart each way	434	30 feet apart each way	48
11 feet apart each way	360	35 feet apart each way	35
12 feet apart each way	302	40 feet apart each way	28

RULE—Multiply the distance in feet between the rows by the distance the plants are apart in the rows, and the product will be the number of square feet for each plant or hill, which, divided into the number of feet in an acre (43,560), will give the number of plants or trees to the acre.

Plums

Plum trees are often called the poor man's tree because they require so little room to grow and are always such prolific bearers. The markets demand for high-grade plums is almost unlimited, and for dessert, cooking, and canning, no fruit is more delicious.

Use plum trees to fill the places on your farm where other fruit trees will not have room to grow. Plant a commercial orchard of plums; give it good attention and it will bring you large profits and prove a good investment.

BURBANK JAPANESE PLUMS

PLUMS—Continued

A light, sandy soil is preferred for plums, but they do well in almost any soil as long as it is well drained. The tree should be sprayed annually with Bordeaux mixture.

The varieties we offer have been thoroughly tested and are "stand-bys." They may be relied upon to furnish annual crops of highly profitable and delicious fruit. The stock is clean, healthy, and sturdy two-year-old, budded on the finest Myrobolon plum stock.

	Each	10	25
2 year old, 3 to 4 ft.	$ .75	$7.00	$16.25
2 year old, 4 to 5 ft.	.90	8.50	20.00
2 year old, 5 to 7 ft.	1.25	12.00	27.50

PLANT SPRING OR FALL, 16 TO 20 FEET APART

GERMAN PRUNE

GERMAN PRUNE—One of the oldest varieties. The tree is vigorous in growth and productive. Large, purple fruit that is firm, sweet, and delicious. A freestone. September.

LOMBARD—A favorite for canning and culinary purposes. Of medium size, oval, violet-red. Flesh is yellow, juicy, pleasant and good. Adheres to the stone. Good market variety. The tree is strong and productive, bearing when quite young. Ripens late in August.

One or two plum trees of several varieties added to your order, or, if your space does not allow more than a single tree, will be an investment that will repay you a thousand fold in the quantity of the fruit produced.

Spring Hill Nurseries, Tippecanoe City, Ohio.

Gentlemen:

Received the trees Saturday evening. They are surely fine. Best I have ever received and have bought from several different places. I thank you for the careful packing and will want to get some Apple trees soon.

Yours very truly,
LEONARD MILLS,
New Madison, Ohio.

MOORE'S ARCTIC—Purplish black plum with a thin bloom. The fruit is small to medium; flesh juicy, sweet and fine flavored. Tree is healthy, a regular and abundant bearer. August.

REINE CLAUDE—Fine variety for canning. Fruit is large, roundish oval, greenish yellow, spotted with red; flesh yellow, juicy, rich, and of the finest quality. Very productive.

SATSUMA—Ripens in early September. Purple red. Flesh dark red. Tree a free bearer, but should be planted in situation which may be slightly protected by buildings or a windbreak.

SHIPPER'S PRIDE—A large, showy plum, frequently reaching a diameter of two inches. It is dark purple in color, of the Damson type. The flesh is sweet and firm. Good shipper. September.

YELLOW EGG—A beautiful yellow, egg-shaped plum of the largest size; the flesh is yellow, and somewhat coarse; always clings to the stone. This is an excellent variety for canning and always brings a good price on the market. The tree is a prolific bearer and a good grower. Late August.

ABUNDANCE—A beautiful yellow, heavily overspread with purple-carmine; large to very large; the flesh is yellow, very juicy, sweet and quite firm; skin tough. The tree is a strong, thrifty grower, very hardy and prolific. The fruit stands shipping well to distant markets. July.

BRADSHAW—Remarkably good early plum. This variety is a very large, dark violet red. The flesh is yellow, juicy and good. A valuable market variety. The tree is an erect, vigorous grower. Middle of August.

BURBANK—Successful almost anywhere. The fruit is of very large size, the color cherry red, mottled. The flesh is yellow, sweet and firm. It is fine for keeping and shipping. The tree is a vigorous grower, but so straggling that it requires sharp pruning. Ripens in August.

LOMBARD

Grapes

One of the most satisfactory crops that can be grown, because it can be depended upon practically every year. Grape vines will grow almost anywhere, but to produce the finest specimens they should be carefully cultivated and pruned. A south or southwestern exposure will, as a rule, give best results. The soil should be dry, and if not naturally so, should be artificially drained before planting.

A top dressing of well-rotted manure should be applied each year, alternated every few years with a dressing of slacked lime.

Grapes can be easily trained over fences, buildings, arbors, summer-houses, pergolas, etc., and in this way are ornamental as well as useful. The enemies of the grape vine and fruit are very few and can be easily kept in check.

DELAWARE RED

PRICES OF LARGE SELECT GRAPE VINES
30c each; $2.75 for 10; $6.25 for 25; $23.00 per 100.

Your selection of any of the following kind. We prepay all transportation charges on orders of $4.00 or more. This means when your order amounts to $4.00 or more of any kind of stock. Plant spring or fall, 8 to 10 feet apart.

AGAWAM—Large, compact, dark red or maroon colored berries. Ripens early and is very attractive.

BRIGHTON—A very desirable, early red grape. Berries are medium to large sized bunches, good flavor and quality.

CATAWBA—Medium large, red grape, of good quality. Late.

CAMPBELL'S EARLY—One of the strongest growers and a most hardy variety. Quality is good and is a long keeper.

CONCORD—The most popular black grape in America. Good shipper, sweet and juicy. Vine is hardy, healthy and productive.

DELAWARE—This is an American grape. There is no other variety more delicately flavored or having a more agreeable aroma than the Delaware. Next to the Concord, it is the most popular, and has a beautiful pink color.

MOORE'S EARLY—A very popular, early grape. Hardy and a good grower.

NIAGARA—When fully ripe the berries are a greenish yellow. Skin tough with quality similar to the Concord. This is the leading white grape for home and market use.

POCKLINGTON—The berries are a golden yellow, sweet and juicy. Vine hardy, and good producer. Ranks next to the Concord. Good shipper.

SALEM—A strong, vigorous vine; berries large, dark copper color, sweet, with a thin skin. Early September.

VERGENNES—The large, white amber berries are rich and delicious, and hold firmly to the stem. An excellent keeper.

WOODRUFF RED—A very profitable grape grown with the Delaware. Good shipper and keeper. Very vigorous and good producer.

WORDEN—A seedling of the Concord. Large bunches, which ripen ten days earlier than the Concord. This variety deserves a good place on the market and should be planted in every garden.

WYOMING—Vine very hardy, healthy and robust. Berries a beautiful light red; nearly double size of Delaware. Flesh tender, sweet, juicy. Best early red market grape.

CONCORD GRAPE

COLLECTION NO. 13
For Spring 1921 Only.
25 Grape Vines No. 1 Plants all for $5.20
Parcel Post All Charges Paid.
Following Varieties:

10   Concord—Black
5   Niagara—White
5   Moore's Early—Early black.
5   Agawam—Red

One crop of fruit will many times pay you for your investment on the above. Vines are guaranteed as to quality and purity—you are taking no chances.

Currants

Experience teaches that a cool, moist soil is best adapted to the growth of currants. Strong, moist loams, with a considerable mixture of clay, are good. Even, well-drained, stiff clay will give good results.

The pruning is simple, but very important. The younger the wood, the finer the fruit. It is absolutely necessary, however, that a fair supply of the old wood be left in order to insure productiveness. No wood over three years old should be allowed to remain. Plants should be set in rows six feet wide and about three feet apart in the row. Twenty-five hundred can be planted to the acre.

Plant Spring and Fall, 3 to 4 feet apart.

2-year old, first-class plants, 35c each; $3.50 per 10; $8.50 per 25.

CHERRY—Bush a strong grower, very hardy, and quite prolific bearer. The large, bright red berry has a thin skin and a fine flavor.

FAY'S PROLIFIC—The leading market currant. One of the best known varieties and universally used by the large fruit-growers. Long stems, fine flavor, and very productive. Fruit easy to pick, good shipper; plants are very hardy.

LONDON MARKET—Bush vigorous and upright. One of the best for northern climates and at the same time a leader in the Southern states. Beautiful dark red berries medium sized with large branches. A favorite for home, market and will stand long shipments.

RED CROSS—A strong-growing, very productive variety. The medium-sized, bright red berries are borne in long clusters and are of the finest quality.

WHITE GRAPE—One of the most vigorous growing varieties we have. Fruit excellent for table use, having a mild acid flavor. The golden-white berries are borne in large, handsome clusters.

WILDER—Upright and vigorous grower, bright red berry of excellent quality; ripens and remains bright and firm very late. Largely planted by the best fruit growers. It is our first choice of all the kinds.

FAY'S PROLIFIC

WHAT PARCEL POST MEANS

Just because we say "Parcel Post" does not mean the plants are small. The vines offered in all collections are strictly first class, good, big plants, same size and quality of all plants offered in catalogue. If you cannot use all the plants yourself, you can sell a few to your neighbors. They would be glad to plant a few and would pay 35 or 40 cents for them and that would be cheap.

The "Kant-Klog" Sprayer

SPRAYS TREES, FRUITS AND VEGETABLES, DISINFECTANTS, WHITWASH AND MANY OTHER USES.

"Kant-Klog" Nozzle. The only nozzle that can be successfully cleaned without stopping the spray or removing nozzle from the tree. The only nozzle ever made to give both flat and round sprays or solid streams.

Spring Hose Cock. A slight pressure starts the spray. Remove it and spray stops instantly. Saves time, labor and fluid.

DIRECTIONS

A few seconds' working of the air pump thoroughly agitates the solution and charges the sprayer with compressed air. This being a very powerful and elastic force will, as soon as the thumb presses the "Shut-off," force out the liquid in the form of either a spray or a solid continuous stream as desired. After sprayer is charged you need not stop for anything; just walk along from one row to another, the machine will supply sufficient spray to enable you to work as fast as you can walk. The great saving in time, labor and solution even on small sprayings will more than pay for this splendid machine the first month it is used, to say nothing of the big increase in crops as a result of spraying properly.

Price, as described above, with galvanized steel body, brass air pump, hose, escape valve, "Kant-Klog" nozzle, thumb pressure Spring "Hose Cock" and carrier strap, $8.00. Polished brass body with same attachments, $11.25.

Brass Pipe for elevating nozzle in tree spraying. Several can be screwed together when necessary. Three feet long, 80c.

Gooseberries

DOWNING

One of the hardiest of the bush fruits. The best results are obtained by planting gooseberries in moist, but not soggy, clay loam; but they will do reasonably well in any well-drained soil if they are well fertilized once each year. The gooseberries bear most freely on two and three-year-old wood. Therefore, the aim should be to keep a continuous supply of vigorous shoots. Prune freely to encourage upright growth. We offer all first-class plants.

DOWNING—One of the most favored of all gooseberries for family use and a very good market berry. Medium sized fruit; flesh soft and juicy. This variety is planted more extensively than any other kind by the fruit growers.

HOUGHTON—Very productive, good and vigorous grower, an old and reliable variety; very hardy.

JOSELYN—Of English type, very good grower, large-sized berries, very productive, affected somewhat with mildew through America.

2-year-old, first-class plants, 40c each, $3.50 per 10, $7.50 per 25. Plant Spring and Fall 3 to 4 feet apart.

> The Medical Authorities of the world say "Fruits are a necessity as well as a luxury, and should form a part of the food regime of every person. At our prices everyone can have fruit.

Rhubarb

Plants 15c each, $1.00 per 10, $7.50 per 100.

LINNAEUS—Leaf-stalks long, large, tender, juicy, produced quite early. Cellar-grown rhubarb with beautifully pink, tender stalks may be enjoyed in March by anyone who will devote a little time to it. For this crop the plants are grown from spring until fall in very rich soil so as to establish a number of crowns on each root. In the fall a number of roots are packed together with rich soil in some cool, dark cellar. After the crop has been cut, the roots are replanted in the garden to regain their vigor for the next year's forcing.

LINNAEUS RHUBARB

Keep Your Trees Healthy

SPRAY YOUR TREES WHILE THEY ARE DORMANT. Use Scalecide or Lime and Sulphur

Have you trees bear fruit of quality. Keep your trees healthy and growing. Proper spraying at proper times with proper material, will produce healthy trees to bear quality fruit that will bring highest prices. Scalecide and Lime Sulphur is the proper spray material, is not poisonous to man or beast, mixes instantly with water when stirred, and stays mixed. Write for prices and other literature on spraying.

Put up in following packages. Prices on request

Dry Lime and Sulphur	Dry Arsenate of Lead
100 lb. drums.	
25 lb. drums.	100 lb. drums.
10 lb. packages.	50 lb. drums.
Scalecide	12½ lb. drums.
50 gal. barrels.	5 lb. packages.

> **FREIGHT AND EXPRESS CHARGES PREPAID ON ANY ORDERS IN THIS CATALOGUE ON ORDERS AMOUNTING TO $4.00 OR MORE.**

Asparagus

PRICES OF ASPARAGUS PLANTS

$1.00 per 25; $3.00 per 100; $12.50 per 1,000

Plant 1 to 1½ feet apart.

It is not necessary to tell the good qualities of the asparagus, as it is known to everybody. It is the most healthful and delicious of the early vegetables. It is very easily grown, and no plant will produce as the asparagus does with as little outlay. May be either planted in fall or spring. Dig up the ground deep, put on plenty of well-rotted manure, thoroughly mixed in the soil, throw out a bed about four to five inches deep, lay the plants in by spreading the roots out well, and scatter the dirt over the plants about four inches, or the depth of the ground thrown out, press the dirt well around the plants by patting it down with a spade or shovel, then top-dress the ground with about three inches of well-rotted manure and scatter salt enough over the top of this to make the ground white enough to track a rabbit. The second year after planting, you will be able to harvest enough asparagus for a good sized family from a bed of about two hundred plants. Two hundred plants will make a bed three feet wide and fifteen feet long. Keep the crown of the asparagus cut regularly so it will not get too large and woody. A good asparagus root properly planted will produce from three and one-half to seven pounds of asparagus, and when planted in small beds, where it can be well mulched and cared for, will even do much better than this. It is necessary to start with good roots. It depends much more on the care taken of the plants and the plant food given them than it does the variety planted. Salt should be put on at the end of every season, in the spring of the year.

BARR'S MAMMOTH—A very good variety with large, even sized roots.

CONOVER'S COLOSSAL—Really colossal. Deep green shoots from one to two inches in diameter are sent up thickly from the crowns.

PALMETTO—In large markets, this asparagus brings the highest prices on account of the size and beautiful appearance of its stalks. Some years it is on the market several days before the other varieties.

PALMETTO
ASPARAGUS

Strawberries

Price, per 100, $1.50; per 500, $7.00; per 1,000, $10.00. Plant 1 to 1¾ feet in rows 4 feet wide.

DUNLAP   AROMA   GLEN MARY

Strawberries are so well known and generally grown that it is hardly necessary to give much space to descriptions. If interested in knowing about the culture of strawberries, we will be pleased to send our booklet, "What, Where, When and How to Plant," which tells about preparing bed, cultivation, etc. We will only give here a few notes of general importance.

Ground must be well drained. Ground must be well prepared. Plant in spring—always the best time. Generous supply of well-rotted manure is a great benefit. Protect plants when received from nursery; never allow roots to be exposed to the sun or wind. Plant in rows four feet apart and eighteen to twenty-four inches apart in row. Crown of plant should never be below surface of ground.

AROMA (Per)—One of the finest for long-distance shipping. The large berries are bright red to the center. Of conical shape, with prominent yellow seeds that help to make them very attractive on market. The quality is such that it is a leader with many growers.

BRANDYWINE (Per.)—A well-known variety that has proven very successful wherever planted. Produces immense quantities of large, very fine deep red berries that have a delightful flavor. The bright yellow seeds make a fine color contrast with the beautiful red fruit. This is one variety that has been a favorite in most all of the States east of the Rocky Mountains and also on the Pacific coast. The foliage of this variety is very large; the fruit stems strong and erect, holding the large berries well off ground. We can freely recommend this as being one of the very best berries.

BUBACH (Imp.)—This variety has never failed to win a reputation wherever planted. It is famous for its beautifully colored, large berries and mammoth crops. It is a leader among the money-makers, an old, well-tested variety that has never failed.

ENHANCE (Imp.)—A very good bearer for the market. The plant is a healthy and vigorous grower, reliable, productive, and of a good quality.

FENDELL (Imp.)—A comparatively new variety; seedling from the Wm. Belt, originated in 1915 by Charles E. Fendell. It is noted for the strong growing plants, extra large, fine-flavored berries, and great productiveness. It has a record of better than sixteen thousand quarts per acre.

GANDY (Per.)—Another old favorite. Its popularity, instead of decreasing, is steadily increasing. The fruit is dark red with dark red seeds. A very large berry that does best on a heavy clay soil. Considered one of the best shippers ever known and has done well wherever tried. Should be planted with the Senator Dunlap, as fertilizer.

GLEN MARY (Per.)—Midseason. Unexcelled as a long-distance shipper and one of the best for our States, as it resists dry weather admirably. A heavy bearer of large, delicious fruits.

HAVERLAND (Imp.)—On account of the hardiness, wonderful productiveness of the plants, and the general appearance, good shipping qualities, and excellent flavor, this berry continues to grow in popularity. It has always proven to be one of the best varieties wherever planted, and thrives best with the Senator Dunlap as fertilizer.

HERITAGE (Per.) — The plants of this variety are good growers. The fruit is unusually large for one that continues to bear throughout the berry season.

NICK OHMER (Per.)— Medium to late fruiting. A most popular sort with berries of beautiful carmine color. The fruit is large, firm, and of unusually delicate flavor. The long stems make picking very easy. A fine shipper and suitable for fancy market. A leading variety with many growers.

SENATOR DUNLAP (Per.) —The demand for this variety has been increasing steadily, as it has an unusually long fruiting season. It bears immense quantities of large, handsome, rich, fine-flavored, dark red berries, which are of uniform size and shape and very attractive appearance. The demand for this variety

GANDY

among fruit growers shows that it is coming to the front as one of the best.

UNCLE JIM (Per.)—Is a strong grower that bears large fruit of a rich color. One of the best for canning; a good market variety and a good shipper. Heavy producer. Every strawberry patch should contain some of this variety.

UNCLE JIM

PLANTS THAT
GROW
Express Prepaid
On All Orders of
$4.00 or More.

Fall Bearing Strawberry Plants

Fall-bearing Strawberries are a success. Every home especially should have a patch of these, enough for home use at least. There is good money in them, if raised for market. Just think of fresh strawberries all through the fall months. What a luxury! You can have all you need of them by planting some of the following varieties.

Set the same as other strawberry plants and keep the fruit stems picked off till about July 1, same as on all new set plants. They will produce a good paying crop of berries the first year.

Seventy-five cents per 12; $3.00 per 100, $11.00 per 500.

PROGRESSIVE (Per.)—A wonderful fall-bearing strawberry, as the spring-set plants not only produce big crops of berries the same season, but the runner plants also begin to bear fruit as soon as they are set, and in this way Progressive yields a crop of fruit the first year. Fruit good size, smooth, of good color and appearance. Progressive will please you.

SUPERB (Per.)—The best and most profitable fall-bearing strawberry grown. Superb berries are much larger than other varieties and of far better quality and better appearance. After the first year, they produce a big crop in June and again in the fall. It is the best known and most widely planted. The plants are strong and stand the winter well. The fruit is large, round, rich, dark colored, glossy and attractive.

SENATOR DUNLAP

CUTHBERT, A STANDARD RED

Raspberries

Many improvements in the hardy varieties of Raspberries, make the cultivation of the fruit compartively easy. They will do well in any good soil, but thrive best in deep, moist (not over-wet) soil. The lighter loams are preferable for the red varieties, while the heavier suits the black varieties best.

Pinch back the black varieties early when the young canes are about three feet high, in order to keep the bushes snug and compact. Mulching will prove beneficial to both varieties, both in summer and winter. Once the raspberry patch is established it requires very little cultivation. Plant Spring and Fall, 3 to 5 feet apart.

GROWN FROM TIPS

CARDINAL—One of the most vigorous growers and one of the hardiest of all the raspberries. In fact, it is considered one of the very best purple berries. The best proof of this is that nearly all growers discard the other purple varieties after the Cardinals are once established. They produce a fine quality of dark red or almost purple berries thru a long season. A very fine quality for family use. 25 for $1.00; 100 for $3.50; 500 for $15.00.

CUMBERLAND—The fruit of this variety is largest of all the black caps; firm, a good shipper, and one of the most profitable as a market berry. Very choice black cap. 25 for $1.00; 100 for $3.50; 500 for $15.00.

GREGG—Known for many years by more people than is any other raspberry on the market. Large, showy, black, firm, and will ship well. Hardy and vigorous grower. Ripens about midseason. 25 for $1.00; 100 for $3.50; 500 for $15.00.

HAYMAKER—Very large, firm berry, good shipper, and one of the best for home use. A lighter red than the Cardinal. Plants are very hardy, and a good crop may be depended upon each year. 25 for $1.00; 100 for $3.50; 500 for $15.00.

KANSAS—Plants are strong, vigorous growers, will stand extremes of drought and cold weather and still bear large crops. These will grow with less care than will any others of the "tip" varieties. 25 for $1.00; 100 for $3.50; 500 for $15.00.

GROWN FROM ROOTS

CALLED SUCKER PLANTS

CUTHBERT—Considered the queen of the market, as they bring a higher price on the market than any other of the red raspberries. The fruit is large, dark crimson, firm, sweet, rich, highly flavored, and as beautiful as strawberries. This is one of the hardiest of the red raspberries and endures the extreme northern climates or the southern summers with equal vigor and productiveness. 25 for $1.00; 100 for $3.50; 500 for $15.00.

MILLER'S RED—A very healthy grower that bears a good quality of bright red berries throughout the entire raspberry season. In fact, during some seasons, they bear fruit as late as August. An excellent shipper. 25 for $1.00; 100 for $3.50; 500 for $15.00.

KING—A very early red berry that always commands a good price. The plants are hardy and productive and the fruit of good quality. The King Raspberry is earlier than any other variety. 25 for $1.00; 100 for $3.50; 500 for $15.00.

J. Fletcher Clark, Eaton, Md., writes: Enclosed find check for $20.00 covering the Staymans Apple trees shipped me. They were fine. Accept thanks for your prompt delivery.

CUMBERLAND

Ever-Bearing Red Raspberry

ST. REGIS. This new raspberry of recent introduction stands in a class alone. It will produce fruit from June until the berries freeze in the fall or early winter. The fruit begins to ripen very early and continues on the new canes throughout the remainder of the summer and fall months.

Berries are a bright crimson, good size, rich, sugary, with excellent raspberry flavor. Flesh firm and meaty, a good shipper. Canes stocky, of strong growth, with an abundance of dark green, leathery foliage.

St. Regis is a heavy bearer and has proven one of the most profitable of the red varieties, also a producer of fruit during the summer and fall. 10c each, 75c per 12, $4.00 per 100.

ST. REGIS RASPBERRY

they can be cultivated, they should be plowed, and in the winter a coarse litter of mulch thrown over them. The vines will grow up through this and keep the fruit from the ground. We are only offering one variety which is considered the best of all Dewberries now in cultivation.

Dewberries

The Dewberry is a trailing or vine form of the Blackberry. May be trained to run over stone piles, over rough embankments or rocky hillsides, and sometimes produce a very large crop of fruit annually over land where no other crop could be grown. The fruit is very large and always at a premium with the commission men or the open market. If they are planted where

LUCRETIA—Fruit of high quality and very large, often one to two inches long and one inch in diameter. Perfectly hardy and a great bearer. 10 plants for 50c; 100 plants for $3.00; 500 for $12.00.

Blackberries

All Blackberries, 10 plants, 50c; 100, $4.25; 500, $20.00. Plant Spring and Fall 5 to 7 feet apart. The Blackberry thrives well in almost any soil, but to reach perfection demands a strong loam tending towards clay, rather than sand.

In many parts of the country, winter protection is a necessity and often adds greatly to the yield, where not considered really essential. The blackberry, as a rule, outyields all other members of this family and is usually one of the most profitable to grow when properly managed, providing the climatic conditions are favorable. Planting is best done in the spring. If however, plants are set in the fall, each plant should be covered with a difficult task, yet success depends upon the proper method in the spring. The pruning of the blackberry is not a mulch of earth or straw manure, which should be removed. The old canes should be removed yearly; it is preferable in the summer after they have borne their crop of fruit. Cultivation should be frequent but shallow, as deep cultivation disturbs the roots and induces them to sucker. Pinch back canes when three or four feet high. It is best not to allow more than three or four canes to a hill. ed varieties.

Blackberries should be planted about four feet apart in rows seven feet apart. It will take about 1450 plants to the acre when planted this way. Those offered below are all tested.

AGAWAM—Fruit medium size, jet black, sweet and tender to the core; a valuable variety for home use, being sweet as soon as black.

BLOWER—Originated in the celebrated small fruit belt of Chautauqua Co., N. Y., where it has been thoroughly tested for several seasons. Claimed to be the hardiest, most productive, finest quality, and to bring on the market the highest price of all blackberries. Has produced 2694 berries on one bush, 2720 quarts on one-third acre. Large size, jet black, good shipping properties, best quality, and unexcelled productiveness are main features of this splendid new sort.

EARLY HARVEST—Best easily grown blackberry in cultivation. Fruit, firm, of good quality; excellent shipper, good market variety. Needs some protection in winter.

ELDORADO—This is a comparatively new variety and has proven itself to be the best of all blackberries under cultivation. The best proof for this is the berry growers. After once fruiting Eldorado, they discard almost all other varieties which they have. It is very hardy, claimed to have no equal in this respect. Fruit very large, jet black, good shipper, good quality, and a great producer. We personally recommend this variety above any other that is offered.

SNYDER—Very hardy, great producer, medium size, and one of the best known varieties of blackberries, succeeding wherever planted. Over-production is its greatest fault.

TAYLOR—Berries of fine flavor, larger than Snyder, canes of vigorous growth, iron-clad hardiness, and wonderfully prolific. Ripens late.

BLOWER BLACKBERRY

Edible Nuts Trees

CASTANEA (Chestnut)

DENTATA (American Sweet Chestnut)—A valuable native tree, both useful and ornamental. The timber is desirable and possesses a fine grain for oil finish. They are a remarkable race of trees, bearing very young, and yielding large crops of nuts of extraordinary size. The nuts are sweet, delicately flavored, and are a valuable item of commerce. 3 to 4 feet, 75c each.

CORYLUS (Hazelnut)

AMERICANA (English Filbert)—These nuts grow wild throughout a good part of the United States. The nuts are medium size, nearly round, rich flavor of superior quality. The cultivation of these nuts is not very profitable. 2 to 3 feet, 50c each.

CARYA (Hickory)

PECAN—Pecan growing is becoming a favorite industry in the Southern and Western States and is quite profitable. The trees are long lived, quite hardy and productive. A species of hickory which may well rank first among our native nuts. They are large, thin-shelled, full kernels, and of rich flavor. Seedlings, 2 to 3 ft., 75c each.

JUGLANS (Walnut)

REGIA (English Walnut)—A fine ornamental tree a grows well in the climate of the Middle States and bears freely. Large profits are realized from the orchards of California and the South and still large quantities of these nuts are imported. The nut is about the size of a black walnut; it has a thin shell and contains a large kernel which has a very delicate flavor. 2 to 3 feet, 75c each.

NIGRA (Black Walnut)—This is one of the largest, grandest, and most massive of our forest trees. It is a favorite of the landscape gardener. A very good tree for public planting on account of its rapid growth and handsome foliage. The timber of this tree is very valuable. The nuts are large, round, covered with a thick husk, and the kernel has a fine flavor, much liked by many people. 5 to 6 feet, 75c each.

CINEREA (Butternut, White Walnut) —The tree is especially esteemed for its abundant crops of fruit which abounds in oil and is sweet and rich. The nut is oval; the husk is covered with a sticky gum, and the surface of the nut is much rougher than any of the other walnuts. The tree is valuable as a park tree. 5 to 7 feet, $1.00 each.

SIEBOLDIANA (Japan Walnut)— Large, spreading top of this tree makes it very ornamental. Trees very hardy, having stood a temperature of twenty degrees below zero without injury; begins to bear when three years old. The nuts are larger than the common hickory nut and borne in clusters of from ten to twenty. The shells are moderately thick, the kernels are sweet. Should be extensively planted. 3 to 4 feet, 75c each.

AMERICAN SWEET CHESTNUT

ENGLISH WALNUT

Hardy Ferns

The most beautiful and natural effects can be produced by planting of hardy ferns. They should be planted to be protected from the prevailing winds. They are perfectly hardy and can stand planting either in shady or sunny positions.

The hardy ferns are most satisfactory for planting on shady banks and around porches, where the sun does not reach. They are valuable in that they do well in any good well drained soil and require practically no care.

Ferns have become a feature in all decorations whether for apartments, conservatories, or for tropical bedding in summer. No home should be without them. We can furnish either of the following varieties.

20c each; $2.00 for 12.

OSTRICH FERN—The large leaf, tall growing variety.

ROYAL FERN—One of the large growing varieties.

CINNAMON FERN —Medium grower in height.

A PLANTING OF HARDY FERNS

A SPLENDID EXAMPLE OF A TREE BACKGROUND FOR A HOME

Hardy Ornamental Shade Trees

Ornamental shade trees play an important part in the arrangement of all lawns and parks. They are often invaluable as windbreaks, supply shade, and help retain the moisture—conditions that are essential to the growth of many of the choicest shrubs and perennials.

There are trees noteworthy for their profusion of bloom; some for the unusual color of bark or leaves; and some for the strength of their limbs. Some trees will endure smoke much better than others, making them valuable for city planting.

For many years we have given especial attention to ornamental shade trees, and are confident of our ability to please the most critical buyer. We have the largest variety of this class of stock to be found in this part of the state. Planted in Spring or Fall.

PLANTED IN SPRING OR FALL

ACER (Maple)

GINNALA—A shrub or small tree to twenty feet; leaves three-lobed and beautiful, turning bright red in Autumn. May be used as the Japanese Maples, where they are hardy. 6 to 7 feet, $1.25 each.

NEGUNDO (Box Elder, Ash Leaf Maple)—A large, spreading tree of rapid growth very hardy, and a good drought resister. Largely planted for windbreaks and timber. The leaves resemble those of the ash. 5 to 10 feet, $1.00 each.

PLATANOIDES (Norway Maple)—A large, handsome tree with a compact, rounded head of spreading branches, attaining a height of one hundred feet. The broad, deep green leaves cast a dense, refreshing shade. One of the best and most beautiful trees for the street, park, cemetery, or lawn planting. 8 to 10 feet, $1.50 each; 10 to 12 feet, $2.00 each.

SCHWEDLERII (Purple-leaved Norway Maple)—One of the most beautiful of the shade trees. In early spring the young leaves are bright red, changing to purplish green as they grow older. In autumn, they are golden yellow. The tree has a round, compact head and large leaves which cast a dense shade. 6 to 8 feet, $1.50 each; 8 to 10 feet, $2.50 each.

SACCHARUM (Sugar Maple, Rock Maple)—Large trees to 120 feet with gray bark. Long lived. Grows well except in damp, soggy soils. An excellent street and shade tree of upright, dense growth. Leaves turning bright yellow and scarlet in autumn. 6 to 8 feet, $1.00 each; 8 to 10 feet, $1.50 each.

SACCHARINUM (Soft Maple, Silver Maple)—This is one of the best known of all the maples. It is an ornamental tree with wide, slender, spreading branches. Thrives almost anywhere, but grows very rapidly in moist, rich soil. 6 to 8 feet, 75c each; 8 to 10 feet, $1.00 each.

ACER PALMATUS (Japanese Maples)

The Japanese Maples are trees of dwarf habit and are the most delicately beautiful of all the small exotic trees. They may be planted in masses, or as specimen plants, and for this reason are treated separately. There are many happy variations in these maples, some with delicately cut leaves, some highly colored during the first weeks of summer, while still others are highly colored throughout the entire season.

VAR ATROPURPUREUM—The leaves of this species are a very dark purple, and are especially beautiful in early spring. Very effective grown as specimens or in groups. Sometimes ten feet high. 2 to 3 feet $2.50 each; 3 to 4 feet $5.00 each.

VAR DISSECTUM—A variety with light green foliage, very deeply cut, almost fern-like foliage, of dwarf and pendulous habit. A handsome little tree. 1½ to 2 feet, $3.50 each.

VAR PURPUREUM—The finely cut leaves of this variety are an intense purple. Beautiful. 1½ to 2 feet, $3.50 each.

PLANT TREES THAT GROW Saves disappointment, time and money. Express prepaid on all orders of $4.00 or more.

NORWAY MAPLE

AESCULUS (Horse Chestnut)

GLABRA (Ohio Buckeye)—A large growing ornamental, native shade tree. Valuable for park and street planting. Beautiful leaves with showy, interesting flowers. 6 to 8 feet, $1.25 each.

HIPPOCASTANUM (European Horse Chestnut)—A large growing, ornamental shade tree with beautiful dark green foliage. The white flowers are showy and interesting. 6 to 8 feet, $1.25 each.

AILANTHUS (Tree of Heaven)

GLANDULOSA—A very rapid-growing, open-headed tree, with large, pinnate foliage of bright green color and tropical appearance. Will grow in almost any soil and resists the dust and smoke of cities that prove fatal to many other trees. 10 to 12 feet, $1.50 each.

BETULA (Birch)

Birches not only form an interesting class of trees, but they are also beautiful and ornamental. They are especially desirable for park and other ornamental planting. The bark usually separates into thin, papery leaves. The foliage is rarely attacked by insects. Their graceful habit, slender and often pendulous branches, and their picturesque white trunks, make them conspicuous marks on any landscape.

ALBA (European White Birch)—This tree will attain a height of eighty feet and is a valuable specie. They are especially valuable for planting in colder climates. 6 to 8 feet, $1.00 each; 8 to 10 feet, $1.25 each.

LENTA (Sweet Cherry or Black Birch)—A handsome, round-headed tree with pendulous branches when older. Very attractive in the spring when covered with its long, staminate catkins. The trunk is of dark, reddish brown; the young bark is aromatic and of agreeable flavor. Usually grows sixty to seventy feet in height. 8 to 10 feet, $1.50 each.

POPULIFOLIA (American White Birch)—A small, rapid-growing, ornamental tree, thriving on very poor soil. Bark white and conspicuous in winter. 8 to 10 feet, $1.25 each.

LUTEA (Yellow Birih)—One of the most valuable trees of the Northern States. The bark is silvery gray or orange; on old trees, reddish brown. The young bark is aromatic. 8 to 10 feet, $1.50 each.

CUT LEAF BIRCH

CARPINUS (Hornbeam)

AMERICANA (Hornbeam)—A native tree, in growth quite similar to the beech, but the foliage is thinner and form more irregular. 4 to 5 feet, $1.00 each.

BETULUS (European Hornbeam)—Thick, dense habit and slow growth. Good for screens and hedges. 3 to 4 feet, 50c each; 4 to 5 feet, $1.00 each.

CATALPA

BUNGEI (Umbrella Catalpa)—Just the tree to be used for formal effects. Propagated on a stem of the Catalpa Speciosa. It makes a very unique ornamental tree. It has a broad, dome-shaped head at the top of a long, straight stem. When the tree attains its full growth, the top is often fifteen feet in diameter and not over three to four feet tall on top of a strong stem from five to seven feet high. An exceptionally hardy variety. 5 to 7 feet, 1-year old, $1.50 each; 2-year old, $2.00.

SPECIOSA (Western Catalpa)—A handsome tree with large, bright green foliage, especially ornamental in June when laden with beautiful white flowers in large, showy panicles. Desirable on account of its rapid growth and ability to thrive in a great variety of soils. Valuable for lawn and street planting. 8 to 10 feet, $1.00 each.

CARAGANA (Pea Tree)

ARBORESCENS (Siberian Pea Tree)—A very desirable tree for hedges, windbreaks, or ornamental planting. Of Russian origin. It is hardy and a rapid grower. It has a beautiful foliage resembling the locust, a fragrant bloom. followed by seed pods. Extensively planted through the Northwest. 4 to 6 feet, 50c each.

CERASUS (Cherry)

PADUS (European Bird Cherry)—A small tree which is covered with large, white flowers borne on somewhat drooping, leafy racemes. The fruit is black with a rough stone. 6 to 8 feet, 50c each.

CERCIS (Judas Tree)

CANADENSIS (American Judas Tree, Red Bud)—A handsome ornamental tree growing twenty or thirty feet high. It has a broad irregular head and perfect, heart-shaped, glossy leaves. Beautifully attractive in early spring when the leafless branches and twigs are covered with rosy pink blossoms. Very beautiful and attractive planted as single specimens or in groups. 3 to 4 feet, 30c each; 4 to 5 feet, 80c each.

CORNUS (Dogwood)

FLORIDA (White Dogwood)—Handsome tree of medium size, flowering after red buds when most other trees are still bare. Grea, white flowers are three inches across, lasting in favorable weather for several

CATLAPA BUGEI

weeks. The bright red bark on its young branches makes it cheery in winter. Blooms when small. 2 to 3 feet, 60c each; 3 to 4 feet, 80c each.

FLORIDA (Var Rubra)—A very beautiful form of the dogwoods with blossoms that are pink on the southern side. 3 to 4 feet, $1.05 each; 4 to 5 feet, $1.50 each.

CRATAEGUS (Thorn)

COCCINEA (Scarlet Fruited Thorn)—A fine native variety; blooms in May, producing a profusion of white blossoms, succeeded by red fruits; large leaves. 2 to 3 feet, 40c each; 3 to 4 feet, $1.00 each.

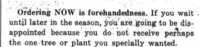

RED BUD
THE FIRST SPRING BLOOM

Ordering NOW is forehandedness. If you wait until later in the season, you are going to be disappointed because you do not receive perhaps the one tree or plant you specially wanted.

While we try to grow sufficient to more than supply our customers' needs it sometimes happens that certain plants and trees are largely demanded and our stock becomes exhausted early in the season.

You need have no fear that plants or trees will be sent before the opening of the planting season. YOU may set the date you wish to have them arrive or we will advise on receipt of your order the time that our experience has taught us is the best time to plant.

We can't emphasize this point too strongly— Order early and avoid disappointment.

CRATAEGUS (Continued)

COCCINEA FLORE PLENO (Paul's Double Scarlet Thorn)—Of quick growth, showy, and perhaps the best sort. The large, perfectly double flowers in May are a rich, glowing crimson. 4 to 5 feet, $1.50 each.

CORDATA (Washington Thorn)—A very desirable specie with beautiful fall coloring and large clusters of bright red fruits, remaining on the branches a long time. Formerly much used for hedges. 2 to 3 feet, 75c each; 3 to 4 feet, $1.25 each.

CRUS-GALLI (Cockspur, Thorn)—A very decorative specie of distinct habit, handsome in bloom and showy, bright red fruits that remain on the branches a long time. The leaves assume a bright scarlet and orange in fall. 2 to 3 feet, 75c each; 3 to 4 feet, $1.25 each.

OXYACANTHA (May, English Hawthorn)—A small growing, attractive tree, bearing in early May an abundance of white, sweet-scented flowers, followed by bright red fruits. Much used for hedges in England. 2 to 3 feet, 75c each; 3 to 4 feet, $1.25 each.

DIOSPYROS (Persimmon)

VIRGINIANA—This tree is much grown for its decorative features. An ornamental tree with a round-topped head and handsome, shining foliage. This fruit is the well-known, puckery persimmon of peculiar flavor, of a pale orange yellow, with a bright red cheek, when touched by the frost, which is necessary to bring it to full ripeness. 3 to 4 feet, 75c each; 4 to 5 feet, $1.00 each.

ELEAGNUS (Olive)

ANGUSTIFOLIA (Russian Wild Olive, Oleaster)—Highly ornamental small tree, with handsome, silver-green leaves. The flowers are small and inconspicuous, but fragrant. The fruit is yellow, coated with silver scales. Valuable for planting in dry or cold places. 2 to 3 feet, 50c each; 3 to 4 feet, 75c each.

FAGUS (Beech)

We especially recommend the beeches for ornamental and park planting because of their great beauty and enduring character. When planting, be careful to prune severely and judiciously, leaving a good supply of well-developed buds. Beeches that are branches to the ground are the best shape for screens.

GRANDIFLORA (American Beech)—A noble, native tree of large size and round, spreading habit. Attractive at all times but especially so in winter and early spring when the bark is grayish white. The medium-sized, triangular-shaped nuts are sweet and fine flavored. 6 to 7 feet, $1.50 each.

PURPUREA—A strong, vigorous tree with beautiful purple leaves. Should have one in every park, cemetery, or lawn. Trees should be planted of the sizes of three to four feet. They are easy to transplant at this size, but are very hard to grow if transplanted when larger. 2 to 3 feet, $1.50 each; 3 to 4 feet, $2.25 each.

FRAXINUS (Ash)

AMERICANA (American White Ash)—A handsome, hardy, broad-headed, quick growing shade tree, sometimes reaching 120 feet in height. Very valuable in landscape work, for park and street planting. 6 to 8 feet, $1.25 each.

GYMNOCLADUS (Kentucky Coffee Tree)

CANADENSIS—Clean, stout, and free from disease; in every way a desirable shade tree for city streets or lawn planting. The blunt, twigless branches make the tree especially interesting in winter. The tropical-looking foliage does not come out until late, about the middle of May. 6 to 8 feet, $1.00 each.

GINKGO (Kew Tree)

BILBOA (Maiden Hair Tree)—A tall sparsely branched, usually slender tree, attaining sixty to eighty feet in height. Especially valuable for solitary planting to secure picturesque effects; growing in favor as a street tree because of upright habit and their freedom from insect injury. Leaves are fan-shaped. 6 to 8 feet, 85c each; 8 to 10 feet, $1.50 each.

KOELREUTERIA (Varnish Tree)

PANICULATA—The Koelreuterias are medium-sized, rather sparing-branched, round trees with light green, pinnately divided leaves and small yellow flowers in large, terminal panicles appearing in summer and followed by bladder-like pods. Hardy as far north as Massachusetts. It stands drought and hot winds well. 6 to 8 feet, $1.25 each.

LIQUIDAMBER (Sweet Gum)

STYRACIFLUA—One of the most ornamental trees in the Middle or Northern States. Beautiful at every stage. Its habit adapts it to street and park planting, under which conditions it succeeds well. Insects and diseases never bother it and it also withstands salt air. 30 to 40 feet. 4 to 5 feet, $1.00 each; 6 to 8 feet, $1.50 each.

LARIX (Larch)

The Larches are ornamental, deciduous, coniferous trees, chiefly grown for their bright or light green, feathery foliage and regular habits. 4 to 6 feet, 75c each; 6 to 8 feet, $1.00 each; 8 to 10 feet, $1.50 each.

AMERICAN WHITE ASH

DECIDUA (European Larch)—A pyramidal, coniferous tree, remarkable for its beautiful light green foliage in early spring, expanding with the first warm days of the advancing season. Grows to a height of 100 feet. 4 to 6 feet, 75c each; 6 to 8 feet, $1.00 each; 8 to 10 feet, $1.50 each.

LEPTOLEPIS (Japan Larch)—The foliage when young is a bright green, changing to a bright golden yellow in autumn. Sometimes eighty feet. 4 to 6 feet, 75c each; 6 to 8 feet, $1.00 each; 8 to 10 feet, $1.50 each.

LARICINA (American Larch, Tamarack)—A tree to sixty feet, with horizontal branches, forming a narrow, pyramidal head; bark reddish brown, leaves of a light green. 4 to 6 feet, 75c each; 6 to 8 feet, $1.00 each; 8 to 10 feet, $1.50 each.

LIRIODENDRON (Tulip Tree)

TULIPFERA (Yellow Wood)—A tall, handsome, hardy, ornamental tree of pyramidal habit and rapid growth. It has clean foliage of light, bluish green appearance, which is rarely attacked by insects. In June, its tulip-shaped, fragrant flowers of a creamy yellow and orange color, are very numerous. A distinguished tree for park, avenue, and lawn planting. 6 to 8 feet, $1.00 each; 8 to 10 feet, $1.50 each.

MAGNOLIA

The magnolia is one of the most profuse blooming trees. Especially is this true of the Chinese and Japanese sorts. Magnolias are not easily transplanted and we move them with small balls of earth attached. Since most of them bloom when only a foot or two high, there will be no long waiting for flowers. Transplant in spring only.

MAGNOLIA ACUMINATA (Cucumber Tree)—A rapid-growing, pyramidal tree, attaining a height of

TULIP TREE BLOSSOMS

from sixty to ninety feet, with large, deep green leaves that turn yellow in autumn; in midsummer the dark foliage is given a spangled effect by the appearance of the large, creamy white flowers, which are succeeded by cucumber-shaped fruits, at first green, later deep scarlet. A grand avenue tree. $2.00 each.

MAGNOLIA TRIPETALA (Umbrella Tree)—The common name has its origin in the peculiar whorled arrangement of the large, lossy leaves; a native species that is both hardy and vigorous. The giant white blossoms, four to eight inches across, open in June and are followed by oblong, rose-colored fruits. It attains a height of about forty feet. $2.50 each.

SWEET or WHITE BAY (M. Glauca)—A slender tree or very large shrub, evergreen in the south. The leaves are oblong or oval, shiny green on top and nearly white underneath; flowers creamy white, fragrant and cup-shaped, two to three inches across, blossoming for several weeks in spring and early summer.

PAULWONIA (Empress Tree)

A tree with immense, large leaves that produce a decidedly tropical appearance. The large panicles of blue trumpet-shaped flowers are sweet-scented and appear in June. When winter-killed, the stems may be cut to the ground and new ones will soon grow up. 3 to 4 feet, $1.00 each.

POPULUS (Poplar)

BOLLEANA (Bolle's Poplar)—A very tall, narrow-topped tree with cottony leaves rather deeply lobed. 6 to 8 feet, $1.25 each.

EUGENEI (Eugene Poplar, Carolina Poplar)—One of the surest, most rapid growing trees. It will grow where other trees appear weak and starved. The leaves are glossy and fresh looking. Valuable for quick effects. 8 to 10 feet, 75c each; 10 to 12 feet, $1.25 each.

NIGRA (Var. Italica)—One of the characteristic trees of Italy. With age, the Lombardy Poplar becomes one of the most striking and picturesque trees, particularly when some of the sprouts are allowed to grow about the old stock. Excellent for landmarks. 6 to 8 feet, 50c each; 8 to 10 feet, $1.00 each; 10 to 12 feet, $1.25 each.

PLATANUS (Sycamore)

OCCIDENTALIS (American Sycamore, Buttonwood)— Similar to the Oriental Sycamore, but claimed to be little

LOMBARDY POPLAR

more affected by smoke at some places. Also leaves claimed to fall off a little earlier in the fall. 6 to 8 feet, 75c each; 8 to 10 feet, $1.00 each.

PRUNUS (Plum)

PISSARDI (Purple-leaved Plum)—A distinct and handsome little tree, covered with a mass of small, white flowers in spring, large, showy, pinkish-purple leaves that deepen in color to the end of the season. It is perfectly hardy wherever the common plum will stand, and is unique and beautiful ornament to the lawn at all times of the year. 3 to 4 feet, 75c each.

PYRUS (Flowering Apple)

FLORIBUNDA—A small tree often thorny, covered with beautiful rose-red flowers about the time the leaves appear. The fruit is small, red, and borne on long, slender stalks. 3 to 4 feet, $1.00.

AUGUSTIFOLIA (Bechtel's Flowering Crab—The most beautiful of the flowering crabs. The tree rarely grows over twenty-five feet, and blooms when quite young. At a distance, the fragrant, delicate pink flowers look like dainty little roses. 3 to 4 feet, $1.50 each.

HALLEANA (Parkman's Flowering Crab)—A dwarf or small tree growing from six to fifteen feet high. Its beautiful flowers are rose-colored, half-double, and hang on slender, reddish pedicels. The fruit is small, brownish red, and ripens quite late. In every way a beautiful tree. 3 to 4 feet, $1.00 each; 4 to 5 feet, $1.50 each.

QUERCUS (Oak)

Possibly no other species of trees equals the oak in all its characteristics; certainly, none compare with it in enduring majesty. No tree is better suited to large estates or roomy lawns where there is plenty of room for its development. In many places it is gaining favor for avenue and street planting, but its complete adaptability is not yet established. **All Oaks**, 6 to 8 feet, $1.25 each; 8 to 10 feet, $2.00 each.

COCCINEA (Scarlet)—A noble tree attaining a height of eighty feet, with gradually spreading branches which form a rather open head. It grows and does well in

PENTANDRA WILLOW.

dry situations. Especially beautiful in the fall when the leaves turn to a brilliant scarlet.

PALUSTRIS (Pin Oak)—A handsome tree, especially when young. Often used for avenues; grows rapidly, prefers a somewhat moist soil. The foliage turns bright red in fall. Tree is fibrous rooted and transplants well.

ROBOR, var. **Pedunculata** (English Oak)—A long-lived tree with stout, spreading branches forming a broad, round-topped head. The leaves are dark green and somewhat smaller than those of our native species. A handsome tree for lawn or public grounds.

ALBA (White Oak)—The White Oak is one of the noblest trees of the Northern States and a beautiful park tree where space will allow it to be fully developed. The foliage assumes a beautiful, deep, vinous, red or violet-purple color in the fall.

RUBRA (Red Oak)—Beautiful oak of rapid growtr, growing into a large, majestic tree, with usually broad round head, the foliage turning to dark red in the fall.

SALISBURIA (See Ginkgo)

SALIX (Willow)

DISCOLOR (Pussy Willow)—A shrub or short-trunked tree; foliage smooth, bright green above and whitish beneath. Worthy of more extensive cultivation. Thrives on dry ground. The catkins of this specie are one of the earliest harbingers of spring. 6 to 8 feet, 75c each.

PENTANDRA (Bay-leaf or Laurel-leaf Willow)—Shrub or small tree to twenty feet. Foliage bright shining green and the branches chestnut color. 4 to 5 feet, 75c each; 8 to 10 feet, $1.25 each.

VITELLINA, var **Aurea** (Golden-bark Willow)—The branches of this variety are a beautiful golden yellow and very attractive in the winter, but especially so in early spring. 8 to 10 feet, $1.25 each.

SORBUS (Mountain Ash)

AUCUPARIA (European Mountain Ash)—An ornamental deciduous tree with beautiful foliage which turns orange-red in the fall. The fruits are showy and often remain all winter, if not eaten by the birds. Not particular as to soil. 6 to 8 feet, $1.25.

SYRINGA (Lilacs)

JAPONICA (Japan Lilac)—This variety of the lilac was introduced from Japan where it attains the height and dignity of a small tree. The foliage is abundant and of a feathern texture. Flowers white and appear in large terminal panicles a month after the other lilacs have bloomed. 3 to 4 feet, 75c each.

PALUSTRIS OAK

TAXODIUM (Cypress)

DISTICHUM (Deciduous Cypress, Bald Cypress) —A tall, deciduous tree, growing 150 feet high, bark light cinnamon-brown, branches erect, forming a narrow, pyramidal head, which at maturity is broad and rounded, with slightly pendulate branches. Leaves narrowly linear, acute, thin, light-green. 6 to 8 feet, $2.00 each; 8 to 10 feet, $3.00 each.

TILIA (Linden)

AMERICANA (American Linden, Basswood)—A beautiful, rapid-growing tree with large, broad leaves and fragrant flowers. The bloom furnishes the best of bee pasture. The linden should be extensively used as a lawn tree; it is also very valuable for park and street planting. It thrives in moist, rich soil, but does well in any good soil. 6 to 8 feet, 75c.

PLATYPHYLLOS—This is the broad-leaved linden of the European plantations and it is probably the largest of all. The leaves are large and the flowers appear earlier than some of the varieties. 6 to 8 feet, $1.00.

VULGARIS—Small-leaved European linden. This species grows nearly as large as the preceding one. The leaves are smooth and green on both sides. This is the celebrated species of Berlin. It blooms about a week to ten days earlier than the American linden. 6 to 8 feet, $1.25.

ULMUS (Elm)

Elms are considered the best of all the street trees and are used in greater quantities than probably all other kinds of varieties combined. In planting Elm, do not crowd them. They produce very fine trees, fine shaped heads, and live for centuries. All our Elms for ornamental or street purposes, are well rooted, nice, straight trunks, with well formed heads.

AMERICANA—Very valuable for park planting, for avenues, and as a shade tree for lawns. One of the most majestic and graceful of our shade trees. Hardy, a rapid grower, resists drought well, and is long lived. 6 to 8 feet, 75c each; 8 to 10 feet, $1.25 each; 10 to 12 feet, $1.50 each.

CAMPESTRIS (English Elm)—This tree is planted as an avenue tree. The foliage remains green several weeks later than those of the American elm. 8 to 10 feet, $1.50 each.

The quality of stock this year is as good as can be grown. We are keeping prices as low as possible, and will be in a position to give you quality, service and pack in good condition. We guarantee our stock to be good, clean, healthy trees, and they are the very best that can be had at any price. We want your business, and will appreciate same, but we can't promise you everything until we get your order then forget the promises, as you know is often done. We prefer doing more than we promise. We will promise you this, we will give you 100 cents value on every dollar.

Evergreens

Hardy coniferous evergreens are indispensable in much of the landscape work that is done today. Every lawn, park, etc., should have at least a few of these beautiful specimens to give the bit of color that is needed to set off the rest of the planting. They are especially valuable as backgrounds against which to group other trees and plants with beautiful colored leaves and branches. They are useful for screens and windbreaks and, besides this, furnish homes for birds that remain with us during the winter.

Right here let us call your attention to the fact that many of the very best varieties are scarcely known at all to the great mass of people. We have grown in our nurseries over one hundred varieties that are all hardy and well adapted to the various uses that are now being made of evergreens.

> Our evergreens have all been several times transplanted, so have a fine root system. With this they will readily establish themselves when planted on the lawn or elsewhere.

ABIES (Fir)

BALSAMEA (Balsam Fir)—An ornamental evergreen that is very hardy. The fragrant leaves are dark green above and pale beneath. For ornamental purposes it is unexcelled. Grows rather rapidly when young. Requires good drainage. 2 to 3 feet, $1.50.

NORDMANIANA (Nordman's Fir)—One of the most beautiful of all evergreens. Dark green foliage above, with silvered white below the leaves. Thrives well in any soil, but desires a slightly protected position. Fine for specimen plants. 2 to 3 feet, $2.00 each.

JUNIPERUS (Juniper)

COMMUNIS, var **Hibernica** (Irish Juniper)—A narrow, columnar form, with upright branches, deep green, tips of branchlets erect. 2 to 3 feet, $1.50 each.

CHINENSIS, var. **Pfitzeriana**—A tree forming a broad pyramid with horizontally spreading branches. 2 to 3 feet, $3.00 each.

SABINA (Savin Juniper)—A low, wide-spreading, thickly branched evergreen shrub, rarely ten feet high. 15 to 18 inches, $1.50 each.

SABINA, var. **Tamariscifolia**—A low, procumbent evergreen; the needle-like leaves usually appear in groups of three, slightly in-curved, dark, and bright green, with a white line above. Extremely hardy. 15 to 18 inches, $1.75 each.

VIRGINIANA (Red Cedar)—This evergreen attains a height of one hundred feet, with conical head and spreading or upright branches. The leaves are spiny pointed. 2 to 3 feet, $1.25 each.

GLAUCA—A vigorous growing form of the Junipers, with glaucous foliage. Very desirable. 18 to 24 inches. $2.50; 2 to 3 feet, $3.00.

VAR. SCHOTTII—A dwarfish, dense, pyramidal form with bright green and light foliage. 3 to 4 feet, $3.00.

PICEA (Spruce)

ALBA (White Spruce)—A very ornamental tree similar to the Norway Spruce. One of the best for cold climates. Is an upright, compact grower, and retains its branches to the ground. It can be distinguished by its grayish-blue color and quick growth. It matures while comparatively young and lives to a good old age and is altogether very desirable. 2 to 3 feet, $1.00.

EXCELSA (Norway Spruce)—This tree is extensively planted in many of the States. It is of rapid growth, with graceful habits and dark green foliage. It is one of the best conifers to plant for shelter and windbreaks. 18 to 24 inches, 50c; 2 to 3 feet, 80c.

ORIENTALIS (Oriental Spruce)—An exceedingly graceful spruce with dark, glossy foliage. It is of slow growth, therefore valuable for small gardens. It holds its lower limbs for many years and eventually attains the height of 120 feet. 18 to 24 inches, $2.50.

PUNGENS (Colorado Blue Spruce)—A handsome and very hardy tree of symmetrical habit, with light, sometimes almost silvery white foliage. Good in landscape work. 18 to 24 inches, $2.50.

VAR. COMPACTA—A dwarf, compact form, originated in the Arnold Arboretum. Light green foilage. 12 to 18 inches, $2.50 each.

KOSTERI (Koster's Blue Spruce)—The best of the blue spruces. Perfectly hardy and may be grown anywhere but thrives best in moderately moist, sandy soil. A most attractive tree on account of its silvery blue foliage, which densely crowds the branches. 2 to 3 feet, $4.50 each; 4 to 5 feet, $10.00; 5 to 6 feet, $15.00.

PINUS (Pine)

AUSTRICA (Austrian Pine)—This species is very popular for grouping or as specimens. A very tall, massive tree, with heavy, plumed, spreading branches and rather stiff, dark green needles. Most of these species make a vigorous growth when young and when older they are very picturesque. Should be planted when young from the nursery row. 2 to 3 feet, $1.00; 3 to 4 feet, $1.50.

STROBUS (White Pine)—A valuable, ornamental, hardy pine, of rapid growth, symmetrical when young, picturesque in old age. No tree is better adapted to break up a monotonous sky-line of plantations in Northern parks. 2 to 3 feet, $1.00 each; 3 to 4 feet, $1.50.

SYLVESTRIS (Scotch Pine)—This grows to be a large tree, seventy to one hundred and twenty feet in height, with spreading, somewhat pendulous branches, pyramidal when young, with broad and round top, often picturesque head in old age. Quite hardy. 2 to 3 feet, 75c each; 3 to 4 feet, $1.50.

MONTANA, var Mughus (Dwarf Mountain Pine)—This pine is very valuable in habit, with dark brown branches, bright green leaves, stout and acutish. The cones are ovate, a light gray in color, surrounded by a blackish ring. The tree is broader than it is high, forming a dark, dome-shaped bush. Very effective for rocky places. 12 to 18 inches, $1.25; broad specimen plants, 24 to 30 inches, $4.00.

PONDEROSA (Jack Pine)—One of the tallest and most important of the pines of the Western States. Hardy as far north as New York. The branches are stout, spreading, and often pendulous. 2 to 3 feet, 75c each.

PSEUDOTSUGA (False Tsuga)

TAXIFOLIA (Douglass Spruce)—This is the tallest and one of the important forest trees of western North America. It would be difficult to overrate its beauty. It probably grows faster than any other conifer. Very desirable for grouping. 2 to 3 feet, $2.00; 3 to 4 feet, $3.50 each.

RETINOSPORA (Cypress)

PLUMOSA, var Aurea (Golden Japan Cypress)—

AUSTRIAN PINE

This is a very striking and useful evergreen in many ways, as it is one of the very few really golden evergreens. It makes a strong and effective contrast with the darker foliage of other evergreens. It is low branched and a very vigorous grower and is unsurpassed for effect in grouping. 18 to 24 inches, $1.00; 2 to 3 feet, $2.50.

PISIFERA (Swara Cypress)—A tall-growing tree with horizontal branches; branchlets flattened, and somewhat pendulous. One of the best Retinospora, being highly ornamental and well known. 2 to 3 feet, $2.50 each.

PLUMOSA, var Aurea—The young growth of this variety is a beautiful golden. Very desirable. 1½ to 2 feet, $2.00 each.

OBTUSA NANA GRACILIS COMPACTA—A dwarf, compact form of the Retinospora Obtusa with fine foliage and graceful habit. Very desirable variety. 12 incses, $2.00 each.

TAXUS (Yew)

BACCATA (English Yew)—A most desirable, dark green foliaged plant, suited for single specimens or for grouping. 2 to 3 feet, $3.00; 3 to 4 feet, $4.50.

CUSPIDATA, var Brevifolia—This is a dwarf, very compact form of the yew, with leaves shorter than the type. 2 to 3 feet, $3.00; 3 to 4 feet, $4.50.

THUYA (Arborvitae)

OCCIDENTALIS (American Arborvitae)—The foliage is of a light green color. This is a very good tree for grouping, for tubs and vases, and for formal uses they are unsurpassed. They are very quick growers and may be trimmed to any desired height. Fine for hedges. 2 to 3 feet, $1.00 each; 3 to 4 feet, $1.50 each.

VAR PYRAMIDALIS (Pyramidal Arborvitae)—Forms a tall, slender column of densely branched, dark green foliage. A very graceful tree having a number of uses. 2 to 3 feet, $1.50 each; 3 to 4 feet $2.50 each; 4 to 5 feet, $5.00 each.

VAR. SIBERICA (Siberian Arborvitae)—A pyramidal tree, lower and denser than the type, with stout branchlets. Foliage bright green all the year. A very desirable sort. 18 to 24 inches, $1.25 each.

VAR GLOBOSA—A dense, dark green form of the arborvitae, growing naturally in globe form. Dwarf habit. 15 to 18 inches, $1.00 each.

VAR. LUTEA (George Peabody's Golden Arborvitae)—This well known variety of the Golden Arborvitae is very handsome and desirable. Very useful in mass planting. 2 to 3 feet, $3.50 each.

NORWAY SPRUCE

VAR. VERNABNEANA—Of smaller and denser habit than the type. Branchlets are smaller with yellowish foliage, bronzy in winter. 3 to 4 feet, $4.00 each.
ORIENTALIS (Biota Orientalis)—A pyramidal tree finally attaining a height of twenty-five feet, very compact form. The foliage is bright green. 18 to 24 inches, $1.00 each; 2 to 3 feet, $1.50 each.

TSUGA (Hemlock)

CANADENSIS (Hemlock Spruce) This is one of the most graceful and handsome of the evergreens and is especially valuable for hedging of evergreens, windbreaks, and for specimen planting. The lumber of this tree is much used for frames of buildings. Finally attains a height of seventy to eighty feet. 2 to 3 feet, $2.50; 3 to 4 feet, $4.00.

Tell us what you would like to plant and we will tell you the best varieties to order.

Many of our customers plant the home grounds but are in doubt as to the best varieties to use. There may be something about the climate or the soil that demands consideration. It is our business to know what, where, when, and how to plant every variety of tree, shrub, vine, or plant we catalogue, and this knowledge is always at the service of our friends.

Put your problems up to the men who KNOW. We are always glad to answers questions.

When placing the evergreen order, we advise having the trees dug with a ball of earth attached to the roots and burlap around the roots, thus protecting them at all times.

PYRAMIDAL ARBORVITAE

Weeping Trees

The weeping trees are very interesting as well as beautiful and effective when rightly placed upon the lawn, or in the park. The charm of these trees is not their stateliness and grandeur so much as it is the odd and fantastic shapes which they so often assume. The best and most satisfactory are offered below.

ACER (Maple)

SACCHARINUM, var Wieri (Wier's Cut-leaf Weeping in Maple)—This variety of the maple has very pendulous branches and the leaves are deeply cleft, giving them almost a fern-like appearance. 8 to 10 feet, $1.50 each.

BETULA (Birch)

ALBA, var. Pendula Lanceolate (Cut-leaf Weeping Birch)—Many attractive characteristics combine to make this a tree of wonderful grace and beauty. Tall, slender, drooping branches and delicately cut leaves. It colors brilliantly in the fall. Its bare white trunk and branches make a beautiful winter picture. 5 to 6 feet, $1.25 each; 6 to 8 feet, $1.75 each; 8 to 10 feet, $2.25 each.

MORUS (Mulberry)

ALBA, var. Tartarica Pendula (Tea's Weeping Mulberry)—We recommend this as one of the thriftiest, hardiest, and most beautiful of the weeping trees, with slender, willowy branches that sweep the ground, forming a beautiful tent of green. 2-year heads, $2.50 each.

ULMUS (Elm)

SCABRA, var. Pendula (Camperdown Elm)—One of the most distinct and picturesque of the weeping trees. Hardy everywhere, and not particular as to soil. The leaves are large, glossy, and dark green. Its vigorous branches have a uniform habit. $2.50 each.

SALIX (Willow)

ELEGANTISSIMA—A strong and the most vigorous grower of all the weeping willows. Used for planting in low places or on the banks of streams, springs, lakes or ponds, making a very beautiful effect. 6 to 8 feet, 75c each.

DOLOROSA (Wisconsin Weeping Willow)—A weeping tree of rarely more than forty feet in height. The branches are long, slender, and pendulous. The trees are quite hardy and will stand planting in the northern States. 8 to 10 feet, $1.00.

TEA'S WEEPING MULBERRY

Trees That Grow
Express Prepaid

The most valuable purchase you can make.
If you have not already our book of "What, Where, When and How to Plant," write for it and it will be sent to you free of charge.

Hardy Deciduous Shrubs

A walk with nature in her undisturbed retreats will soon reveal to her student and lover that she has been most lavish with certain species of shrubs in the various localities. These varieties are frequently good to be used when beautifying the home surroundings, but aside from these, many other varieties are always needed to add variety and many times to aid in making up the succession of bloom.

In many ways nature may be followed. It has been noted among other things that isolated specimens are seldom if ever to be found. Here we learn to plant in masses or groups for best results. Do not delay another season in planting at least some shrubs; for they add materially to the beauty and attractiveness of any home or public place.

Shrubs provide material of a permanent character for the adornment of property at less cost and more effectively than anything else.

ALMOND. See Prunus.

ALTHEA. See Hibiscus.

AMORPHA (False Indigo)

FRUTICOSA (Bastard Indigo)—An interesting ornamental shrub of spreading habit with fine, feathery foliage, remarkable for the unusual color of its dark violet-purplish flowers. 35c each; 4 for $1.00.

ARALIA

SPINOSA (Hercules Club, Angelica Tree, Devil's Walking Stick)—A shrub sometimes growing to forty feet in height. The stout, prickly stems, large leaves, and the enormous clusters of flowers, give this species a very sub-tropical appearance. 50c each; 3 for $1.25.

BERBERIS (Berberry)

BERBERRY—These beautiful shrubs are very valuable for planting in the shrubbery border or for hedges. They readily adapt themselves to almost any location.

MAHONIA, var **Aquifolia** (Holly-leaved Mahonia)—One of the evergreen glories of the ornamental gardens. It has deep green spines at set places; showy, bright-colored yellow flowers in early spring, followed by small berries of a bluish color. Very effective in grouping with deciduous shrubs, perennials, etc. The foliage is similar to our Christmas holly. Very effective for table decorations. 18 to 24 inches, $1.00 each; 3 for $2.00.

THUNBERGII (Japanese Berberry)—Of all the berberries in cultivation, this one is probably the best known, the most planted, and the most effective. It is one of the valuable introductions we have received from Japan, and is especially to be desired because of its low, dense, horizontal growth, bright fall coloring leaves, and the brilliant red berries that remain fresh and attractive until the following spring. It is quite hardy and will thrive equally well in shade or in sunny locations. Especially valuable for planting along walks and drives and for massing in the border. 12 to 18 inches, 25c each; 18 to 24 inches, 30c each; 2 to 3 feet, 35c each.

BUDDLEIA

VARIBILIS MAGNIFICA (Butterfly Bush)—This shrub of comparative recent introduction has grown into favor almost immediately. It is a semi-herbaceous plant, by which we mean in some latitudes it will die down to the ground; and while

BUDDLEIA, or BUTTERFLY BUSH

perfectly hardy, we recommend covering the roots with manure, leaves or other suitable material as winter approaches, as it will help to produce a heavy growth the next season. It is very hardy; blooms the first season, usually from June until frost; the blossoms are borne on long, graceful stems, which terminate in tapering panicles of lilac-colored flowers that are of miniature size, the flower head is frequently ten inches long. 40c each; 3 for $1.00.

CALYCANTHUS (Sweet Shrub)

OCCIDENTALIS—A hardy ornamental shrub with handsome, glossy foliage and very attractive with its flower balls appearing late in summer. It thrives in any good garden soil, but does best in a sandy, moist location. Grows from four to six feet high and is distinctly ornamental. 40c each; 3 for $1.00.

FLORIDUS—A hardy, unique shrub, with large, handsome foliage, and most sweetly scented flowers of a dark reddish-brown. The old-fashioned "shrub" of our grandmother's garden. One of the earliest to bloom in the spring. 40c each; 3 for $1.00.

CARYOPTERIS (Blue Spirea)

MASTICANTHUS—Ornamental, woody plants grown in their lavender-blue flowers profusely in late summer and autumn. Not altogether hardy, as the tops frequently winter kill almost to the ground, but will throw up numerous shoots that will flower the same season. Not strictly a spirea. 50c each; 3 for $1.25.

CEPHALANTHUS (Button Bush)

OCCIDENTALIS—A good-sized native shrub, bearing globular heads of white flowers in July. Delights in a wet soil, but will thrive on upland. 40c each; 3 for $1.25.

CHIONANTHUS (White Fringe)

VIRGINICA—Another very desirable large growing shrub, bearing racemes of fringe-like white flowers late in May. Its purple fruit is highly ornamental, as also the lustrous foliage. 2 to 3 feet, $1.00 each.

CLETHRA (Sweet Pepper Bush)

ALNIFOLIA—A native shrub, to four feet, bearing profusely spikes of yellowish-white scented flowers in August. 40c each; 3 for $1.25.

CORYLUS (Hazel Nut)

AVELLANA (European Hazel Nut)—See Nut Trees.

ATRO PURPUREA (Purple Hazel Nut, Purple Filbert)—Leaves, when first expanded, a deep purple,

CALYCANTHUS (Sweet Shrub)

DEUTZIA, PRIDE OF ROCHESTER

fading as the season advances to a lighter shade. Valuable in the shrubbery border. $1.25 each.

COTONEASTER

HORIZONTALIS—Low shrub. The many branches are almost horizontal. The pink flowers appear in June and are followed by bright red fruits. Very effective. 2 to 3 feet, 40c each; 3 for $1.00.

CORNUS (Dogwood)

MASCULA (Cornelia Cherry)—Hardy ornamental shrub, or small tree of dense growth, with glossy leaves; very attractive in early spring with its yellow flowers and again in the fall with its scarlet fruits. 2 to 3 feet, 40c each; 3 for $1.00.

FLORIDA—A hardy native shrub with handsome foliage, often assuming a brilliant fall coloring; large, white, showy flowers appearing in May before the leaves. 3 to 4 feet, 4 for $1.75; Each, 50c.

SANGUINEA (Red Twigged)—A handsome shrub growing from ten to twelve feet high with purple or dark blood-red branches. Flowers greenish-white in dense cymes. The fruit is black. 2 to 3 feet, 40c each; 3 for $1.00.

ELEGANTISSIMA—This is a beautiful plant. The leaves marked with white. Very showy. 2 to 3 feet, 50c each.

VAR. SPATEH (Variegated Leaf Dogwood)—This variety is especially showy and desirable in the shrubbery border. Leaves variegated with yellow. 50c each. 18 to 24 inches.

ALBA, var Siberica (Siberian Dogwood)—Tall shrub with bright, coral-red branches, making them very ornamental, even after flowers are gone. 2 to 3 feet, 40c each; 3 for $1.00.

CYDONIA (Quince)

JAPONICA (Japan Quince)—Common garden form, growing from three to six feet with spreading, spiny branches. The scarlet-red flowers appear before the leaves and are followed by globular fruits from one and one-half to two inches high, yellowish-green. 2 to 3 feet, 40c each; 3 for $1.00.

CRATAEGUS (See Trees)
DESMODIUM (Tick Trefoil)

DEUTZIA

An elegant species of strong, erect-growing shrubs, except the dwarf sorts. Especially prized for the beautiful clusters of blossoms in May.

PRIDE OF ROCHESTER—Showy, early, large-flowering sort; blossoms in May before others. Grows 6 to 8 feet high. White flowers, large and double. One of the best of the Deutzias. 3 to 4 feet, 40c each; 3 for $1.00.

LEMOINEII—Spreading shrub to three feet in height. Its pure white flowers appear in broad panicles. A very desirable shrub, more vigorous and with more showy flowers than some of other forms. Excellent for forcing. Very hardy. 18 to 24 inches, 50c each.

GRACILIS—A handsome, dwarf, and bushy little shrub with slender, often arching branches. A neat shrub that blooms in May, clothing its branches in pure white flowers. Valuable for shrubberies or for forcing. 12 to 18 inches, 50c.

DIERVILLA (Weigelia)

An ornamental and popular class of graceful shrubs. The beautiful, trumpet-shaped flowers appear in May and June in such profusion as to almost completely hide the foliage. Very desirable for the border and for grouping. They vary in color from pure white to dark red. The following are all choice varieties:

FLORIDA—This is one of the most cultivated species, very free flowering, rather hardy. Flowers pale or deep rose color. 3 to 4 feet, 50c each; 3 for $1.25.

AMABILIS—Vigorous growing shrub, with large leaves and flowers, but less free flowering than the type. Flowers from whitish to pale pink or carmine. May and June. 2 to 3 feet, 50c each.

HYBRID Candida—Very desirable plant for the shrubbery border, with pure white flowers. 2 to 3 feet, 50c each; 3 for $1.25.

NANA VARIEGATA—The leaves of this sort are variegated with white; flowers are nearly white. Dwarf. 2 to 3 feet, 50c each; 3 for $1.25.

EVA RATHKE—Flowers are a deep carmine-red, erect growing. A most profuse bloomer in spring and again in autumn. 2 to 3 feet, 60c each; 2 for $1.25.

ELEAGNUS (Silver Thorn)

LONGIPES—A highly ornamental shrub with handsome foliage and reddish brown branchlets. The flowers are one-half inch long appearing on the lower part of the branches, or on short branchlets; yellowish white, fragrant. The scarlet fruit ripens in June or July, of agreeable, slightly acid flavor. 2 to 3 feet, 40c each; 3 for $1.00.

EUONYMUS (Spindle Tree)

AMERICANA (Strawberry Bush)—An ornamental, upright shrub to eight feet. The flowers appear in June, are yellowish or reddish green, followed by pink fruits that are very attractive. 4 to 5 feet, 75c each.

WEIGELIA, EVA RATHKE

ALATUS (Corky Bark)—An attractive, ornamental shrub to eight feet. The flowers appear in May and June. In autumn the foliage changes to a fine rose color. 2 to 3 feet, 75c each.

EUROPEA—A large shrub to fifteen feet. Covered in the spring with bright yellow leaves, color a beautiful crimson scarlet in fall; stems almost a dark green. 4 to 5 feet, 75c each.

EXOCHORDA (Pearl Bush)

GRANDIFLORA—A well known garden shrub, not often over six to eight feet high. Open habit and with thin, uninteresting foliage. Individual flowers of no value. When in bloom it is dazzling white. The most brilliant shrub of the season. Thrives in any good garden soil. Hardy. Remarkable for the structure of the fruit, which is composed of five small, bony carpels, the central axis in a star-like manner. 2 to 3 feet, 60c each.

FORSYTHIA (Golden Bell)

SUSPENSA—Highly ornamental, free flowering shrub, growing to eight feet; the branches often droop on the ground and taking root. They grow in almost any garden soil and are hardy north. The golden yellow flowers appear in early spring. Excellent for margins or groups. 3 to 4 feet, 40c each; 3 for $1.10.

VAR. FORTUNEI—Similar to the above, but grows with upright or arching branches. 3 to 4 feet, 40c each; 3 for $1.10.

VIRIDISSIMA—Shrub to ten feet with erect, green branches. Leaves very dark green, three to six inches long, the flowers about one inch long, twisted lobes of bright greenish yellow. Less hardy and graceful than the other species. 3 to 4 feet, 40c each; 3 for $1.10.

GENISTA

TINCTORIA (Dyer's Greenwood)—An erect shrub to three feet. It bears golden-yellow blossoms in June and attracts much attention when planted in masses. Good for rockeries and dry hills, or for planting on dry banks. 50c each.

HALESIA
(SILVER BELL)

TETRAPTERA (Snow Drop Tree)—The common snowdrop tree is a

SPIREA VAN HOUTTE, PREDOMINATE

DOUBLE ROSE OF SHARON

fine, small tree, which is covered with a bewildering cloudy mass of small, snowy white flowers, resembling that of the dewdrop, borne about the middle of May before the leaves appear. It is adapted to shrubberies and lawns in almost any position, but prefers a somewhat sheltered place and well-drained rich soil. 75c each; 2 for $1.25. 2 feet.

HAMEMELIS (Witch Hazel)

VIRGINIANA—Hardy ornamental shrub or small tree with deciduous alternate leaves. Petals of flowers are bright yellow, appearing from September to November. It thrives best in moist locations. Valuable on account of blooming at a time when hardly any other shrub outdoors is in flower. 2 to 3 feet, 50c each.

HIBISCUS (Althea)

SYRIACUS (Rose of Sharon)—One of the commonest of the ornamental shrubs, and hardy as far north as Ontario. The shrub is valuable for specimen planting and its bright green leaves an great abundance of variously colored flowers make it very effective, when planted as a hedge. The color ranges from blue-purple to violet-red, flesh color, and white. There are also double forms. The plants we offer are strong, field grown, two and three years old. See Hedge Section for prices on hedge size plants.

Prices—2 to 3 feet, 35c each; 3 for $1.00.

ARDENS—Double violet.

JEANNE D'ARC—Double white.

RUBIS—Single red.

SOUV. CHAS. BRETON—Single violet.

TOTUS ALBUS—Single white.

AULISSIMA—Purple. Shrub form.

BOULE DE FEU—Double red. Shrub form.

MONSTROUS—Double red.

SOUV. CHAS. BRETON—Single violet. Shrub form.

TOTUS ALBA—Single white. Shrub form.

HONEYSUCKLE (See Lonicera)

HYDRANGEA

VAR. STERILIS (Hills of Snow)—Similar to the preceding. Almost all of the flowers are sterile. A very showy variety, excellent for borders. 2 to 3 feet, 50c each.

PANICULATA (Panicled Hydrangea)—A vigorous shrub introduced from Japan; bears long, loose panicles of white flowers. 2 to 3 feet, 35c each; 3 for $1.25.

PANICULATA GRANDIFLORA—This is the best-known form of the hydrangea. A hardy, ornamental shrub to thirty feet with dense, globuse head. The large, white flowers appear in August and September. The sterile flowers changing later to purplish. 2 to 3 feet, 50c each; 3 for $1.25.

TREE FORM—Similar to above, except they are trimmed into the form of a tree. 4 feet, $1.25 each.

HYPERICUM (St. John's Wort)

AUREUM—A showy shrub, three feet high; of stiff, dense habit, top often globular, like a miniature tree; thin, scaling bark. The flowers are a bright yellow during July and August. Adaptable to rocky places, partially shaded, where moisture is retained. 40c each; 3 for $1.00.

ITEA

VIRGINICA (Virginica Willow)—In nature it inhabits low, wet places, but in cultivation will adapt itself to almost any soil. It is not perfectly hardy north, but grows rapidly and endures both sun and shade. Used in the ornamental border, flowers are fragrant and white. 18 to 24 inches, 40c each.

KERRIA (Globe Flower)
Japanese Rose

JAPONICA—One of the first shrubs brought from Japan. It grows from four to eight feet high and as broad as high. Very attractive throughout the year; in winter the light green branches, in early June when the yellow flowers appear in great abundance; and again in autumn when the leaves have changed to a clear yellow. Not quite hardy in the northern states. 18 to 24 inches, 50c each; 3 for $1.25.

VAR. FLORA PLENA—Similar to the above, except that it is more vigorous and more frequent in culture inches, 50c each.

LESPEDEZA (Desmodium)

PENDULIFLORUM (Trefoil)—A very desirable late blooming plant, making a large specimen with age. This is really an herb, throwing up strong, wiry shoots each year from the crown. The stems are reddish brown. The flowers are rose purple, drooping in very numerous, long racemes, which at the top of the plant are panicled. 50c each.

LIGUSTRUM (Privet)

AMURENSE (Amoor River Privet)—Similar in habit to the California Privet, and almost half evergreen. 30c each.

VULGARE (Common Privet)—Ornamental shrub with shiny, dark green leaves. Whitish flowers in June and July, and followed later by black berries which usually remain on the branches through the winter. 2 to 3 feet, 30c each; 5 for $1.00.

TREE HYDRANGEA

(PRIVET—CONTINUED)

IBOTA (Japan Privet)—This is one of the very best of the privets as it is altogether hardy. It will grow ten feet or may be kept trimmed to any desired height as a hedge, and is desirable in the shrubbery border. 2 to 3 feet, 30c each.

VAR. REGELIANUM (Regal's Privet)—A low, dense shrub with horizontal, spreading branches and usually oblong leaves. 2 to 3 feet, 40c each.

OVALIFOLIUM (California Privet)—Handsome shrub, but somewhat stiff habit; foliage dark green, glossy. Excellent for a shrubbery border or hedges. 3 to 4 feet, 25c each.

LILAC (See Syringa)
LONICERA (Honeysuckle)

ALBERTA—A small shrub with slender branches, rigid and spiny in high altitudes. The rosy pink, fragrant flowers are borne on slender and erect stems. May and June. 3 to 4 feet, 50c each.

MORROWI—A very decorative shrub that reaches six feet in height. The beautiful, pure white flowers appear in May or June and are followed by red fruits, which remain until late autumn. 3 to 4 feet, 50c each.

TARTARICA—This is one of the old-time favorite shrubs. It attains about ten feet in height and is extremely easy to cultivate. The pink, white, or cream-colored flowers are produced in pairs. The upper lip is deeply divided and spreading. 3 to 4 feet, 50c each.

TARTARICA, var Alba—This is similar to the above, excepting the flowers are pure white and larger. 3 to 4 feet, 50c each.

FRAGRANTISSIMA—Not quite as hardy as some varieties. It has handsome half-evergreen foliage and blooms very early. Sweet-scented though the flowers are not very showy. 2 to 3 feet, 40c each.

MOCK ORANGE
PHILADELPHUS (Syringa)

GRANDIFLORA—Large, flowering shrub growing to about eight feet, with spreading branches, usually upright and vigorous, flowers slightly fragrant. Rapid grower and most hardy. 3 to 4 feet, 50c each.

LEMOINEII—A graceful shrub with slender, arching branches. The blossoms appear in three to seven-inch short racemes, very sweet scented. 2 to 3 feet, 40c each.

CORONARIUS (Mock Orange)—This is not quite as showy as some of the other species and of somewhat stiff habit, but deliciously fragrant. 3 to 4 feet, 50c each.

VAR. AUREUS—Similar to the above variety except that the foliage is a beautiful golden color. 2 to 3 feet, 50c each.

TARTARICA, BUSH HONEYSUCKLE

BOUQUET BLANC—A real white bouquet of immense size. We can only urge you to include it with your order; we know you will not be disappointed, because it has no equal anywhere. The time, experience, and patience to produce such wonderful plants as these can only be realized by those who have worked with them. 2 to 3 feet, 75c each.

PRUNUS (Almond)

AMYGDALUS, Var. Plena (Double Flowering Almond)—Pink and white varieties. Hardy as far north as Ontario. Flowers very double and appear in early Spring. 2 to 3 feet, 75c each.

CERASIFERA, var Pissardi (Purple Leaved Plum)—One of the best of all purple-leaved trees, holding much of its color in the American summers. It seems to be hardy wherever the common plum it. $1.00 each.

TRILOBA—A most desirable bush. Hardy in central New York and Ontario. The flowers are solitary and mostly rose colored; sometimes white, usually double. The fruit small and red. 2 to 3 feet, 75c each.

RHAMNUS (Buckthorn)

CATHARTICA—A hardy ornamental shrub or small tree rowing to about twelve feet in height, and usually thorny. The inconspicuous greenish flowers appear in auxiliary clusters shortly after the leaves and are followed by black berries. 4 or 5 feet, 50c each.

RHODOTYPHUS

KERRIODES—Sometimes called the White Kerria. A very ornamental, deciduous, much-branched shrub, usually from three to seven feet high. It is very handsome and distinct, and is hardy as far north as Massachusetts. Has bright green foliage. Made very conspicuous by its white flowers in May or June and black fruits in the fall. 2 to 3 feet, 50c each.

PHILADELPHUS OR MOCK ORANGE

RHUS (Sumac)

AROMATICA (Fragrant Sumac)—A good cover plant for dry, rocky banks. Conspicuous in spring for its yellow flowers that are followed by rather bright fruits. 2 to 3 feet, 50c each.

GLABRA, var. Lacinata)—This variety with its deeply and finely cut leaves is very handsome, not quite so hardy as some of the other forms and not so tall growing. 2 to 3 feet, 60c each.

TYPHINA (Staghorn Sumac)—This variety grows in the dryest soils and is a very desirable plant on account of its brilliant fall coloring which, in dry locations, begins to show in August. The crimson fruits remain on all winter. 2 to 3 feet, 60c each.

ROBINA (Locust Acacia)

HISPIDA (Flowering Locust)—This is valued for its elegant clusters of rose-colored flowers, which expand toward the last of May and continue for some time. The branches resemble the Moss Rose. Beautiful for planting in masses. 2 to 3 feet, 50c each.

RIBES (Currant)

AUREUM (Golden Currant)—Most grown for its yellow, fragrant flowers. Fruit dark brown or black. 2 to 3 feet, 60c each.

SAMBUCUS (Elder)

CANADENSIS (Common American Elder)—A valuable genus for the shrubbery family. It grows from five to twelve feet in height. Its flowers are white in flat cymes; the fruit is black and ripens in August. 2 to 3 feet, 60c each.

VAR. AUREA—Same as the above except that the foliage is a beautiful golden color. 2 to 3 feet, 60c each.

LACINIATA (Cut-Leaf Elder)—This is similar to the first variety except that the leaves are variously cut and indented. 2 to 3 feet, 50c each.

SORBARIA (Spirea)

SORBIFOLIA—This is an upright shrub tree to five feet high that closely resembles spireas. The light green foliage is pinnate and the flowers are white. It is a most attractive and interesting plant. 2 to 3 feet, 50c.

LINDLEYANA—Closely allied to Lindleyana Spirea. Well adapted to borders and park planting or on the banks of brooks and rivers. Are liable to crowd out other weaker growing plants. The bright green foliage appears very early in the spring. The white panicles of flowers are quite showy. 2 to 3 feet, 50c each.

STEPHANANDRA

FLEXOUSA—This plant is closely allied to the Spirea style of beauty. It grows two to three feet high and has long, terminal branches which are regularly and densely interwoven in a fan-like manner and are very

SORBARIA SPIREA

graceful. The snow white flowers which appear in June are small, but so numerous that they become very showy. Especially well adapted to theyback of borders. Its foliage during the early spring is tinted red; deep, lossy green during the summer, and in the autumn puts on its usual tints of reddish purple. 2 to 3 feet, 60c each.

SPIREA

There is no more dependable shrub than Spirea. Its graceful foliage and growth and the beautiful blossoms are a delight of the season through.

A selection of varieties planted in masses or rows will assure continuous bloom to the end of summer. The early fall frosts touch the leaves with scarlet, which harmonizes beautifully with the surrounding colors of the fall plants.

Our stock of Spirea is unusually good this year and we have anticipated a large sale of this most desirable shrub. Tell us the effect you want to produce and we will advise kinds. Order early so as to be sure of having the first selection.

ARGUTA—A very vigorous grower and one of the most free flowering and shawy of the early Spireas. Quite hardy. The pure white flowers appear in May. 2 to 3 feet, 50c each.

BUMALDA—Beautiful variety of shrub two feet high, rarely higher, flowers are whitish to deep pink, appearing in July and August. 18 to 24 inches, 50c each.

GOLDEN ELDER

VIBURNUM PLICATUM JAPANESE SNOWBALL

BILLARDIA—A shrub to six feet in height with oblong leaves, usually grayish beneath, at least when young. Flowers are bright pink on five to eight-inch long, tomentose panicles usually rather narrow and dense. July and August. 3 to 4 feet, 40c each; 3 for $1.10.

VAR. ANTHONY WATERER—A very free-flowering, compact, dwarf shrub, with bright crimson flowers in dense corymbs. A very desirable variety that blooms all summer. 12 to 18 inches, 60c each.

CALLOSA—Handsome shrub of low growth, with the young unfolding leaves of a pretty purplish color; flowers small, pale to deep pink in July. 50c each.

REEVESIANA—A very handsome shrub with large, pure white flowers, but only half hardy north. They bloom in May and June and grow to almost four feet in height. 3 to 4 feet, 50c each.

PRUNIFOLIA—Is a graceful shrub, six feet high with slender, upright branches. The ovate leaves are one to two inches long. Flowers are pure white on slender pedicles in three to six-flowered umbels. 2 to 3 feet, 60c each.

VAN HOUTTEI—This is one of the most beautiful or perhaps the most beautiful of the early blooming Spirea, and is quite hardy. It grows to a height of six feet with arching branches that are completely covered with pure white flowers in May. Very effective when planted as a hedge. 2 to 3 feet, 40c each; 3 to 4 feet, 50c each.

THUNBERGII—Five feet high. A very graceful shrub, early flowering. The slender arching branches clothed with feathery; bright green foliage, turning in the fall to orange and scarlet. Almost hardy, but tips of branches are sometimes killed by severe cold. The pure white flowers about one-third across, appearing in April or May. 18 to 24 inches, 65c each.

SYMPHORICARPUS

RACEMOSUS (W a x-berry)—A perfectly hardy shrub from two to three feet high, excellent for massing in the lower parts of a bed or border. The rose-colored flowers appear in loose, often leafy racemes in July and August. The white, waxy-like berries remain on until late in the autumn. 2 to 3 feet, 50c each.

VULGARIS (Indian Currant, Coral Berry)—A rather compact bush valuable because of its abundant and persistent fruit and foliage. 35c each; 3 for $1.00.

SYRINGA (Lilac)

The Lilacs are among the most popular and ornamental of the flowering shrubs, and no garden or park is complete without a collection of them. Some varieties are very fragrant, while others are scentless.

JAPONICA (Japanese Tree Lilacs)—Creamy white. 2 to 3 feet, 75c each.

JOSIKAEA—Single purple. 2 to 3 feet, 75c each.

CHAS DIX—2 to 3 feet, 75c each.

CHARRULEA SUPERBA—Clear blue. 2 to 3 feet, 75c each.

GIANT DES BATTAILES—Single, blue. 2 to 3 feet, 75c each.

LUDWIG SPAETH—Blackish red. 2 to 3 feet, 75c each.

MME. LEON SIMON—Rosy lilac. 2 to 3 feet, 75c each.

MARIE LEGRAYE—Pure white. 2 to 3 feet, 75c each.

MAXIME CORNU—Double rosy-lilac. 2 to 3 feet, 75c each.

TAMARIX (Tamarax)

These plants are very beautiful all the year, in winter for their coloring of the bark and in summer for the light green, feathery foliage and large loose panicles of purplish flowers.

AFRICANA—Is an upright grower to eight feet. Blooms in May. 2 to 3 feet, 50c each.

HISPADA—A graceful shrub with upright branches, flowers pink, appearing in August. 2 to 3 feet 50c each.

PENTANDRA, var Purpurea—Similar to the above except that the flowers are of a purplish hue. 2 to 3 feet, 75c each.

All Shrubs are well developed Plants, 2 to 3 Ft. high or better, except where noted.

VIBURNUM (Snowball)

DENTATUM (Arrow-wood)—A gorgeous, upright, native shrub, thriving best in moist soil. It is especially hardy, doing well from New Brunswick to Minnesota. It blooms in May or June, followed by black fruits. 50c each.

LANTANA (Wayfaring Tree)—This is a hardy shrub, especially for dry situations and limestone soil. The large, white flower clusters open in May and June, and are followed by red fruits. The foliage is particularly soft and heavy. 50c each.

OPULUS (High Bush Cranberry)—Handsome native shrub attaining twelve feet, with rather smooth, light gray branches and stems. The pure white flowers appear in May and June, followed by decorative fruits, which begin to color by the end of July and remain on the branches and keep its bright scarlet color until the following spring. The berries are not eaten by birds. 50c each.

VAR STERILIS (Common Snowball, Guelder Rose)—This is the well known, common snowball of the old-fashioned gardens. Besides the snow-white flowers in May. the foliage is decorative and assumes a bright color in fall. 50c each.

TOMENTOSUM, var Plicatum (Japanese Snowball)—One of the choicest shrubs with much to recommend it and no objectionable features. Foliage is abundant during the summer and fall, and its balls of pure white are borne in great profusion. Fine for specimen planting. 60c each.

Hedge

Among the shrubs for hedges, California Privet takes the lead. It is not particular as to soil, and grows readily in open places or beneath the unnatural conditions of cities, and is one of the best shrubs for seaside planting. Oval-shaped, glossy foliage and pure white flowers in July make it very ornamental. May be pruned back easily to any desired form or shape. The more it is cut, the thicker and handsomer it grows. Our plants are bushy and low-branched—grown especially for hedges.

CALIFORNIA PRIVET—Plants, 18 to 24 inches, $6.50 per 100; 2 to 3 feet, $8.50 per 100.

Larger plants quoted upon request. Express or freight charges prepaid on all orders of $3.00 or more, east of the Mississippi.

IBOTA PRIVET—Excellent for hedges because of its upright habits, beautiful narrow green leaves, clusters of fragrant white flowers, and extreme hardiness. 18 to 24 inches, $15.00 per 100; 2 to 3 feet, $17.00.

AMOOR RIVER PRIVET—Hardiest of all hedge plants. Beautiful upright growth and makes a very compact, beautiful hedge. Sheds its foliage a little earlier than California Privet. 18 to 24 inches, $12.00 per 100; 2 to 3 feet, $16.00 per 100.

BERBERRY, JAPANESE—One of the hardiest and best of hedge plants, growing to four feet. Will adapt itself to all conditions. We advise using 18 to 24-inch plants to transplant. They develop as quickly as larger plants, require less care, and make a better fence. 12 to 18 inches, 20c each; 18 to 24 inches, 25c each; 2 to 3 feet, 35c each.

Evergreen Vines

EUONYMUS (Spindle Tree)

RADICANS—A glossy dark-leaved vine, or it will form a spreading shrub, where it cannot climb. Valuable for covering walls, to which it clings, also for porch boxes. Large, 3-year-old plants, 50c each.

Var. ARGENTEO MARGINATA (Variegated Euonymus)—Same as the above. The leaves are distinctly variegated with white, yellow, and pink shades. Very attractive. Extra large plants, $1.00; smaller plants, 50c each.

HEDERA (Ivy)

HELIX (English Ivy)—A handsome, high-climbing vine with three to five-lobed evergreen leaves. The fruit is black on yellow. The ivy is especially valuable for covering stone walls. Will do well in the shade. 50c each.

—PLANT TREES THAT GROW—

Hardy Climbing Vines

The need of vines for home improvement is well known and there is absolutely nothing that adds more to the beauty of the home than appropriate vines. A porch without a vine is desolate and incomplete. Vines are exceptionally valuable for turning unsightly fences and buildings into things of beauty.

Foliage vines are especially adapted for stone or brick as they look more "at home" than the flowering vines. They are also valuable for working in with flowering vines of poor foliage, because they will form a good background.

There is no class of plants that can be used in so many ways.

AMPELOPSIS

QUINQUEFOLIA (Virginia Creeper)—This is the commonest of the climbers, and at the same time the most useful and the most vigorous growing, doing well in almost any kind of soil. The leaves turn to a bright scarlet and purple in the fall. The dark blue berries remain quite late. 2-year old, 50c ach.

VEITCHII (Boston Ivy)—This vine undoubtedly stands higher in the estimation of the people than any other. After once it is established it grows rapidly and will stay indefinitely, needing only an occasional trimming to keep it within bounds. It is not attacked by disease or insects and the foliage is not injured by the smoke and dirt of cities. The glossy green leaves turn to a brilliant orange-scarlet in the fall. 2-year old, 50c each.

AKEBIA

QUINATA—A hardy ornamental vine of graceful appearance, especially desirable for places in which a very dense shade is not desired. They require a sunny position and well-drained soil. In Japan the fruit, which is very showy, but with us is rarely produced, is eaten, and the stems are used for wicker work. The foliage is never attacked by insects. 3-year plants, 50c each.

BOUSSINGAULTIA

BASELLOIDES (Maderia Vine, Mignonette Vine)— A beautiful, rapid-growing vine with dense foliage. The small white flowers are borne in great profusion and are very fragrant. It is excellent for summer screens and shade for porches. Succeeds best in a sunny position. 5 for 25c; 10 for 40c.

CELASTRUS

SCANDENS (False Bitter Sweet)—Hardy ornamental vine. Very effective by their bright-colored fruit remaining usually throughout the winter. They are valuable for covering trellis-work, trees or rocks and walls. They grow in almost any soil and situation. Fruit is about one-half inch in diameter, orange-yellow, with crimson seed. 35c each; 3 for $1.00.

CLEMATIS

HENRYII—This is a robust plant, a free bloomer, flowers creamy white, becoming fully expanded when grown in the sun. It blooms through August and September. 2-year old, $1.00.

JACKMANII—One of the best known of all the clematises. The velvety-purple flowers, when expanded are four to six inches across, very velvety and distinctly veined. 2-year, $1.00 each.

MAD. ED. ANDRE—This is the nearest approach to a bright red Clematis. It is a very free bloomer and very satisfactory. 2-year, $1.00 each.

PANICULATA—This Clematis is by far the most common of all the species in American gardens. It is extremely showy when covered with the small, white, fragrant flowers which appear late in the season. 2-year old No. 1, 50c each.

LONICERA (Honeysuckle)

JAPONICA, var Halliana (Hall's Japan Evergreen Honeysuckle) —Honeysuckles are well adapted for the covering of walls, arbors, etc., are very ornamental, as the leaves remain on during the winter. The flowers are white, turning to yellow, and are very fragrant. 30c each.

PUERARIA

HIRSUTA (Kudzu Vine)—A hardy vine with large, tuberous, starchy roots, making a most remarkable, vigorous growth of slender, hairy stems. The leaves are variously lobed, vines will grow to sixty feet in a season, producing a profusion of large leaves. In the North the vine dies down to the ground during the winter. 30c each.

WISTARIA

CHINENSIS (Chinese Wistaria)—This is one of the best and commonest of hardy climbers. It has pale green pinnate leaves and bears profusely dense, drooping clusters of purplish, pea-shaped flowers. It blooms in May, and usually gives a smaller crop of blooms in August or September. They will live in rather dry and sandy soil, but prefer a deep, rich earth. 3-year-old, large, 75c each.

Roses

There is probably no flower more popular and better known than the rose. Never was there such a wealth of rose for the amateur to choose from as now. They are being bred for the beauty of the plant form, as well as for the beauty of the flower. It is also bred for health, hardiness, freedom and continuity of bloom. As a result there are some wonderfully beautiful productions, both as to form and color, the latter ranging from pure white through all the shades of pink, red and yellow.

The ideal location for a rose garden is an airy but sheltered spot (sheltered especially from the chilling winds of winter) but exposed all day, if possible, to the sun. A southern exposure is best.

When roses are received, if they seem to be at all dry, soak them in water, being careful at all times not to allow the roots to be exposed to the air. The roses root deeply, therefore the bed should be thoroughly prepared and dug up to a depth of at least two feet.

The roses which we offer below are all good standard varieties, well suited to the home garden, and guaranteed to give satisfaction. Field-grown roses are those that have been propagated in the field and grown from two to three years in the open and are considered more reliable for outdoor planting. To insure success with the roses, follow instructions for making the rose bed given on page 21 of our booklet, "What, Where, When and How to Plant," which will be sent free with all orders, upon request.

These are the hardiest, most persistent to bloom. We recommend them especially for garden culture. They constitute a very important group and embrace a number of varieties. They cover the whole scope in color, size and texture. They are the roses for the amateur as well as for the professional grower.

PAUL NEYRON

HYBRID PERPETUAL ROSES

2-year-old field-grown plants, 75c each; 10 for $7.00.

COQUETTE DE ALPS—A beautiful white rose, tinged with pink. A free bloomer. Very fine.

CLIO—One of the very best. Large, fine, beautiful flesh color, shading to rose in the center. Very vigorous.

DUKE OF EDINBURG—Brilliant crimson scarlet, shaded with maroon. Beautiful.

FRAU KARL DRUSCHKI—The bloom of this rose is perfect in form, on fine long stems of the purest possible white. There is nothing in the line of perfectly hardy roses than can compare with this one in form, color and general appearance.

FISHER HOLMES—Crimson scarlet shaded deeper; large, full and perfect; very beautiful.

HUGH DICKSON—Vigorous free grower and perpetual bloomer with fine foliage; color brilliant crimson. Sweetly scented.

J. B. CLARK—Color is unique among roses, being deep scarlet shaded blackish-crimson with rich bloom like a plum.

MARGARET DICKSON—A white rose, with a rosy flesh colored center that gives a beautiful daintiness to the flower. The blooms are full and solid with curled shell shaped petals. The buds and half-opened flowers are very attractive. The growth is strong and vigorous.

MARSHALL P. WILDER—One of the best hybrid perpetuals. The flowers are large and perfect form, on good length stems, making them very desirable for cut flowers. Color, bright cherry red, changing to carmine.

MRS. JOHN LAING—A soft pink, beautiful form; exceedingly fragrant, and a very free bloomer.

MAGNA CHARTA—Extra large and full, bright rosy pink. A profuse bloomer and very hardy.

MADAM GABRIEL LUIZET—A rich, soft pink rose with deep flesh-colored center; large, full and sweet.

PAUL NEYRON—One of the finest hardy roses ever grown. It blooms unceasingly from June till frost, on thornless stems, with immense, cup-shaped flowers four to six inches across. Color a bright pink.

ULRICH Brunner—Splendid upright grower with bright, healthy foliage. Flowers are good sized and fine form, with well-shaped petals; color cherry red.

CLIMBING ROSES

50c each; 10 for $4.50

CLIMBING AMERICAN BEAUTY—Deep rose carmine center, shaded with rich crimson.

AMERICAN PILLAR—Single pink rose, a new variety.

CRIMSON RAMBLER—Large clusters of small double crimson flowers.

FLOWER OF FAIRFIELD—The same flowers as the Crimson Rambler. Blooms throughout the season.

GRAF ZEPPELIN—Beautiful vivid pink, very hardy.

YELLOW RAMBLER—Yellow rose, very hardy.

HYBRID TEA ROSES

2-year-old field-grown plants, 75c each; 10 for $7.00.

AMERICAN BEAUTY—A well-known variety. Too famous the world over to need a description.

JOHN MOUK—Bright red and salmon pink.

GRUSS AN TIPLITZ—Reddest of all roses. Hardiest of all ever-blooming roses and most profuse bloomer, double.

K. A. VICTORIA—Hardy Hybrid Tea, flesh color; beautiful buds, free bloomer.

KILLARNEY PINK OR WHITE—Very beautiful, flower either in bud or full bloom. Blooms all season, pleasant fragrance. Hardy, will endure most any winter, with a little protection.

RICHMOND—Rich scarlet, free and continuous bloomer. Beautiful rose.

OPHELIA—Salmon pink shading to rose, unusual free bloomer.

SUNBURST—One of the best Tea Roses for bedding.

J. B. CLARK

WICHURIANA, HYBRID CLIMBING, AND TRAILING ROSES

2-year-old field-grown plants, 50c each; 10 for $4.50

DOROTHY PERKINS—Shell pink, beautiful foliage, very hardy.

EXCELSA RED DOROTHY PERKINS—One of the best red varieties, free from all diseases.

Dr. VAN FLEET—Flesh pink, shaded to rose pink in center.

SILVER MOON—White, beautiful foliage, one of the finest.

WHITE DOROTHY PERKINS—Beautiful white Rambler.

ROSA RUGOSA, RUBRA—Valuable, perfectly hardy type, much used in landscape work. Foliage is a lustrous dark green, flowers rosy crimson, borne in cluster, followed by red fruit, which remains all winter.

BABY RAMBLER ROSES

2-year plants, 75c each; 10 for $7.00

Dwarf growing Baby Rambler Roses are very desirable for planting where one wants low growing plants that bloom continually throughout the season.

CRIMSON BABY RAMBLER—Very bright red rose; blooms continually throughout the season.

PINK BABY RAMBLER—Same habit as Crimson with pink flowers.

WHITE BABY RAMBLER—Large clusters of white flowers blooming throughout the season.

AN OLD FASHIONED FLOWER GARDEN IS THE LATEST LUXURY

Hardy Perennials

Hardy Perennials should be planted in spring except where otherwise noted.

Some of these members of the floral kingdom should be found in every flower garden, and many times they add a grace to the shrubbery border that can be obtained in no other way. By a careful choice of varieties, a succession of bloom may be had from early spring until late frost in the fall. They will also furnish cut flowers throughout the entire season.

Planted in the shrubbery border or in beds alone, if judiciously arranged, they will afford greater satisfaction at much less cost than can be obtained by plants procured from the greenhouse that have to be replaced annually.

A perennial bed, to give satisfaction, should be carefully prepared, as it is to remain for a number of years. Many of the plants are shallow-rooted and so the bed cannot be cultivated very much. A good mulch in the fall is always beneficial.

The varieties we offer are all choice specimens and will be much prized for their individual charms.

ACHILLEA (Milfoile, Yarrow)

Hardy, herbaceous perennial for alpine and border effects.

MILLEFOLIUM CERISE ROSEUM—Beautiful cut-leaved foliage. Flowers deep rose colored and good for cutting. Eighteen inches. April to October. 15c each; $1.50 per doz.

BOULE DE NEIGE (Ball of Snow)—Improved Pearl, larger flowers than above variety. Blooms all summer. Slightly more dwarf. Eighteen inches. 15c each; $1.50 per doz.

AGROSTEMMA (Rose Campion)

Erect growing plants with silver foliage, showy flowers. 15c each; $1.50 per doz.

ALBA—Flowers pure white, silvery leaves. July.

ANCHUSA (Sea Bugloss)

Pretty hardy perennial of easy cultivation; prefers a sunny position. 15c each; $1.50 per doz.

ITALICA DROPMORE VARIETY—Gentian-blue flowers that make one of the most desirable of all perennials. Three to four feet.

ANEMONE (Windflower)

One of the most gorgeous of the hardy perennials, as well as one of the most desirable and useful.

WHIRLWIND—Bears large, showy white flowers with a double row of ray florets supported by large dark green leafy branches. Fall. 15 each; $1.50 per doz.

ANTHEMIS (Chamomile)

Heavy scented, continuous bloomer, succeeds in poor soil. 15c each; $1.50 per doz.

TINCTORIA KELWAYII (Golden Marguerite)—Deep yellow flowers and fine cut foliage. Three feet. June to September.

AQUILEGIA (Columbine

Much-prized flower from our grandmother's gardens. The beautiful, long-spurred flowers are borne on thread-like stems well above the bright green divided foliage. Equally at home in sunny or shady locations. Valuable for cut flowers. 15c each; $1.50 per doz.

CANADENSIS (Common American Columbine)—Pretty scarlet flowers, mixed with yellow; long, straight spurs, styles and stamens much protruding. One and one-half feet. April to June.

CHRYSANTHA (Yellow-flowered Columbine)—One of the finest of all the hardy perennials. Flowers are primrose yellow, long spurs. Three to four feet. April to September.

FL. PL.—Double variety of the above.

VULGARIS ALBA PLENA—Double white.

ALBA PLENA—Single mixed. All colors.

ENGLISH LONG SPUR—Beautiful and curious variety of colors.

ARUNDO (Reed)

Tall, leafy perennial grass resembling the bamboo. Five to fifteen feet. 25c each; 5 for $1.00.

DONAX (Giant Reed)—Useful for lawn decoration and to produce tropical effects.

BAPTISA (False Indigo)

Free growing perennial, preferring a sunny location.

AUSTRALIA—A stocky perennial. Two to three feet high. Ornamental foliage. Flowers deep blue and pea-shaped. 15c each; $1.50 per doz.

ASTERS

Perhaps the most popular annual flower grown in this country. Fine for garden and cut flowers.

Hardy Asters in Varieties, 15c each; $1.50 per doz.

ASCELPIOS

Very showy native plants about 2½ feet high, producing their flowers during July and August.

TUBEROSA—Compact umbels of brilliant orange-colored flowers. 15c each; $1.50 per doz.

BELEMCANDA

(Blackberry Lily)

An old garden favorite with orange and red spotted flowers. 15c each; $1.50 per doz.

BOCCONIA (Plume Poppy)

Handsome, hardy perennial with stately habit and finely cut foliage. Especially recommended to grow in an angle of two wolls.

CORDATA—Flowers buff colored, very numerous, borne in large terminal panicles. Five to eight feet. May to August. 15c each; $1.50 per doz.

CALLIRHOE (Poppy Mallow)

Handsome trailing rock or border plant, bearing a profusion of cup-shaped blossoms all summer. Prefers a sunny location. 15c each; $1.50 per doz.

INVOLUCRATA—Loose panicles of large crimson flowers with white centers and cut foliage. Six to ten inches.

CAMPANULA (Bell Flower)

A most important class of hardy plants of easy culture growing either in sunny or shady positions.

MEDIUM (Canterbury Bells)—Very handsome, large numerous bells and panicles. Single and double forms in white, rose and blue. 15c each; $1.50 per dozen.

CHRYSANTHEMUM (Hardy Varieties)

Well known perennials, esteemed for their lavish bloom and exceeding decorative value in late fall. 15c each; $1.50 per doz.

MAXIMUM TRIUMPH—Large white single. Good for cutting. Two feet. June to October.

ALASKA—A splendid form of the Shasta Daisy. The whole plant is gigantic, but compact and graceful; flowers white, four

and five inches across. Very free flowering; small, yellow discs. Good for cut flowers.

RED—

WHITE—

PINK—

YELLOW—

COREOPSIS (Tickseed)

Valuable border plant, because of their profusion of showy, yellow flowers. Much prized for cutting. 15c each; $1.50 per doz.

LANCEOLATA—Flowers golden yellow, hardy and of the easiest culture. One to two feet. June to September.

CLEMATIS

This type of Clematis is deserving of the highest popularity. They form erect bushes 2 to 3 feet high; during their long period of bloom they are very attractive.

DAVIDIANA—A most desirable variety, with fresh, bright green foliage and tubular bell-shaped flowers of deep lavender blue during August and September; deliciously fragrant. 15c each; $1.50 per doz.

DICTAMUS (Gas Plant, Burning Bush)

An ornamental plant of easy culture, valuable for cutting.

FRAXINELLA—Racemes of curious red flowers, with a peculiar color. Worthy of much attention. Two feet, 75c each; $1.50 per doz.

ALBUS—Spikes of attractive pure white, sweet-scented flowers. Valuable for cutting. Two feet. 15c each; $1.50 per doz.

DELPHINIUM

(Larkspur)

Another old-time favorite of the easiest culture. Hardy and prefers sunny, well drained places. Spikes are superb for cutting. 15c each; $1.50 per doz.

BELLADONNA—A sky-blue variety. June to October.

FORMOSOM—The old favorite dark blue with white center; 3 to 4 feet high. Very vigorous, free-flowering and one of the best. 15c each; $1.50 per doz.

HYBRID MIXED—These plants were grown from seed collected from main sorts, and will show some surprising new colors.

DIANTHUS (Hardy Pink)

BARBATUS (Sweet William)—No old-fashioned border is complete without this sweet-smelling, showy flower. 15c each; $1.50 per doz.

HOLBORN GLORY—Various colors, finest strain. 15c each; $1.50 per doz.

CAMPANULA

FOXGLOVE

GAILLARDIA (Blanket Flower)

Probably one of the most universal flowers planted among the hardy perennials. Conspicuous for their profusion of bloom. 15c each; $1.50 per doz.

GRANDIFLORA—Flowers intense, blood crimson, margined with golden yellow. Eighteen to twenty-four inches.

GYPSOHPHILA (Baby's Breath)

A perennial of easiest culture, desirable for massing. 15c each; $1.50 per doz.

PANICULATA—Rough, narrow leaves, very minute white flowers. Graceful. Two to three feet. June.

HELENIUM (Sneezeweed)

AUTUMNAL—Very showy. The flowers are lemon yellow, to rich orange, borne on stems two to six feet. July to October.

RIVERTON GEM—Old gold changing to wall-flower red. 15c each; $1.50 per dozen.

HERMOCALLIS

Popular hardy plants belonging to the Lily family. They succeed everywhere, and should always be included in the border of old-fashioned hardy plants. 15c each; $1.50 per doz.

THUNBERGI—The latest to flower; rich buttercup-yellow, funnel-shaped flowers throughout July. 4 feet.

Fulva—Grows from 4 to 5 feet high, with trumpet-shaped flowers of a neutral orange color with darker shadings; June an dJuly.

DUMORTIERI—Very dwarf; 18 inches; flowering in June; rich cadmium-yellow; buds and reverse of petals bronze-yellow.

HARDY HIBISCUS

Tall growing; especially adapted to backgrounds and shrubbery borders. Of easiest culture, and bloom the entire season. Plants grow 4 to 5 feet tall. 15c each; $1.50 per doz.

MALLOW MARVEL—
MEEHAN—
CRIMSON EYE—
PINK—

HELIANTHUS

The perennial sunflowers are among the most effective hardy plants for large borders for planting among shrubbery, or as clumps on the lawn. 15c each; $1.50 per doz.

IRIS

Among the most desirable and easiest grown of our spring-flowering hardy plants, producing in May, their showy flowers of exquisite coloring of rich and delicate tints.

SIBERIAN BLUE—Purplish-blue flowers, useful for cutting; 3 feet high; 15c each; $1.50 per doz.

KANSAS GAY FEATHER

LIATRIS (Blazing Star, or Gay Feather)—Most showy and attractive hardy perennial native plants. with long spikes of purple and rosy purple flowers from July to Sept.; 3 to 4 feet. 15c each; $1.50 pe rdoz.

IRIS

NEWPORT PINK—Salmony rose color. Eighteen inches. June and August. 15c each; $1.50 per doz.

PLUMARIUS (Hardy Garden or Pheasant Eye Pinks)—General favorite, bearing sweet-scented flowers in great masses during the entire summer. Excellent for cut flowers. One foot high. 15c each; $1.50 per doz.

FL. PL.—Double and single varieties in beautiful colors. 15c each; $1.50 per doz.

DIGITALIS (Foxglove)

GRANDIFLORA—A variety of the old-fashioned Foxgloves, but of more robust habit, larger flowers and longer racemes. The flowers, which are spotted, come in shades of rose and white and are borne in spikes two to three feet high. Separate colors, rose, white, purple, and Vaugh's. 15c each; $1.50 per doz.

ERIANTHUS (False Pampas Grass)

Tall, reed-like perennial, excellent for screens and is one of the best grasses for the Northern States. 15c each; $1.50 per doz.

RAVENNA—The best substitute for Pampas Grass. 4 to 7 feet.

EULALIA (Ornamental Grasses)

Tall perennial grasses, allied to the sugar cane. They are remarkably hardy and excellent for bedding. 15c each; $1.50 per doz.

ZEBRINA—The rather broad green leaves are banded with white. Four to five feet.

FERNS (Hardy)

In a variety of forms and foliage to suit any location. Ferns are usually admired and can be planted to beautify shady and unsightly corners. 15c each; $1.50 per doz.

FUNKIA (Plantain or Day Lily)

The dense stools of foliage are in place along drives or walks. Delight in moist, shady sitpations. The large-leaved varieties are excellent for water-side planting. 15c each; $1.50 per doz.

SUBCORDATA—Similar to the above, dark green foliage. Lilac blue flowers. 15c each; $1.50 per doz.

LANCEFOLIA—Narrow foliage and lilac flowers. 15c each; $1.50 per doz.

ALBO MARGINATA—Flowers white with lavender tinge. Quite large. Leaves large, lined with white along edge. 15c each; $1.50 doz.

IBERIS (Hardy Candytuft)

SEMPERVIRENS—One of the best hardy plants for edging. Pure white flowers. May and July. Six inches. 15c each; $1.50 per doz.

LINUM PERENNE

FLO FLAX—A desirable plant for the border or rockery, growing 2 feet high, with light, graceful foliage and large blue flowers all summer. 15c each; $1.50 per doz.

LYCHNIS CHALCEDONES

All of the Lychnis are of the easiest culture, thriving in any soil, and this in addition to their brightness, has brought them into high favor with lovers of hardy plants. 15c each; $1.50 doz.

CHALCEDONICA—A most desirable plant; heads of brilliant orange-scarlet in June and July; grows 2 to 3 feet high.

MYSOTIS (Forget-Me-Not)

PALUSTRIS SEMPERFLORENS—Blue with yellow throat. Nine inches. 15c each; $1.50 per doz.

ALPESTRIS—More dwarf than the preceding. 15c each; $1.50 per doz.

OENOTHERA (Evening Primrose)

FRUITICOSA YOUNGII—Prized for its stocky growth and continuous bloom of bright lemon-yellow flowers on bold heads. Two feet.

PENSTEMON (Beard Tongue)

Most useful showy perennials, either for the border or rockery. They require little protection. Hardy. 15c each; $1.50 per doz.

BARBATUS TORREYI—Flowers deep scarlet red in spikes. Excellent. Three feet. 15c each; $1.50 doz.

PEONIES

Do much better planted in the fall. Too well known to give description. Red, white, pink, good-sized clumps. 35c each.

PHLOX (Perennial Phlox)

One of the most satisfactory garden flowers. 20c each; $2.00 doz.

PEARL—Late blooming, pure white.

ATHIS—Light salmon pink. Tallest of all.

PANTHENON—Rose salmon. Very large.

P. G. VAN LASSBURG—Purest and largest white Phlox in cultivation. Two to six inches.

PEACH BLOSSOM—Moss or ground pink. Much-et

PEACH BLOSSOM—Peach-blossom pink.

SUBLATA—Moss or ground pink. Much-prized old garden plant, useful for coloring where it is desired to cover ground with a mat. Blooms profusely in spring.

PEARL PHLOX

PLATYCODON (Chinese Bellflower)

GRANDIFLORA—A valuable perennial forming a dense branching bush of upright habit. One to two feet with neat foliage. Blooms from July until frost. Large, bell shaped, deep blue flowers. 15c each; $1.50 doz.

VAR. ALBUM—Same as above except the flowers are white. 15c each; $1.50 doz.

PLUMBAGO (Leadwort)

A pretty dwarf perennial, creeping habit and blooms all summer. Desirable for rock garden.

LARPENTAE (Cape Leadworth)—Deep violet blue flowers. 4 to 6 inches. 15c each; $1.50 doz.

POPPIES

ORIENTAL (Assorted)—These are the regal representatives of this popular genus, growing 3 to 3½ feet high, and far surpassing in splendor of bloom all the annual and biennial kinds. Flowers in May and June. 15c each; $1.50 per doz.

ICELAND (Assorted)—The plant is of neat habit, forming a tuft of bright green fern-like foliage, from which spring, throughout the entire season, a profusion of slender leafless stems 1 foot high, each graced with charming cup-shaped flowers. 15c each; $1.50 per doz.

PYRETHRUM (Persian Daisy)

The pretty, fern-like foliage in the spring, followed by a profusion of handsome blooms in summer, makes the plant very desirable. Unequaled as cut flowers. Hardy under any condition. 15c each; $1.50 doz.

SELAGINOIDES—Beautiful variety with golden moss-like foliage.

AUREUM (Golden Feather)—Yellow foliage.

RUDBECKIA (Cone Flower)

LANCINIATA (Golden Glow)—One of the finest of all perennials. Strong, vigorous growing; produces double, golden flowers in great profusion. 15c each; $1.50 per doz.

PURPUREA (Giant Purple Cone Flower)—Fine, showy, strong-growing variety, with large, reddish-purple flowers, drooping rays, and cone-shaped disc. 15c each; $1.50 doz.

SALVIA (Sage)

Perennials with strikingly orchid-like bloom that makes them welcome in the herbaceous border.

AZUREA (Rocky Mountain Sage)—Sky-blue flowers in great profusion. Six feet. August and September. 15c each; $1.50 per doz.

SEDUM (Stonecrop)

SPECTABLE (Snow Sedum)—Most popular of the Sedums and used for the greatest number of purposes. Rose color to purple flowers. Eighteen inches to two feet. September to October. 15c each; $1.50 per doz.

ATROPURPUREA BRILLIANT—Foliage of a dark, coppery-purple shade. Flowers red. One foot. September and October. 15c each; $1.50 per doz.

STOKES ASTER

A lovely hardy plant producing in abundance handsome lavender flowers and blooming continuously all summer; indispensable for border and for cutting. 15c each; $1.50 per doz. Blue and White.

SWEET ROCKET

The plants grow two feet in height, surmounted by large panicles of brightly colored flowers. 15c each; $1.50 per doz.

PURPLE—

WHITE—

TRADESANTRE

VIRGINICA—Produces a succession of blue flowers all summer. 1½ to 2½ feet. 15c each; $1.50 per doz.

TUNICA (Coat Flower)

Tufted, spreading, hardy, suitable for rockwork, blooming in the summer and fall. 15c each; $1.50 doz.

SAXIFRAGA—Small flowers in great profusion, with rosy-white lilac or purple notched petals. Six to ten inches. July to September.

VALERIAN

Showy plants; grow in any garden soil; do well in the shade. Hardy perennial; grows 2 feet high and blooms the first season from seed. Fine for bouquets. Red and white varieties, 15c each; $1.50 per doz.

VERONICA (Speedwell)

Hardy perennial of easy culture, excellent for growing in shady places and requiring plenty of moisture. Largely cultivated; flowers blue; great favorite. 15c each; $1.50 per doz.

SPICATA—Flowers borne in long, slender racemes, thriving in open soil. Clear blue flowers.

VIOLA (Violet)

Well known plants; hardy perennial, doing best in a cool, moist situation. Seed takes a long time to germinate. Very free blooming, particularly adapted to shady places. 15c each; $1.50 per doz.

MYSOTIS (Forget-Me-Not)

ODORATA (Sweet Scented)—"The queen of secrecy." A very hardy and vigorous variety. The flowers are a pale violet shade, very sweet-scented and blooms until late fall.

YUCCA

Among hardy ornamental foliage and flowering plants this can be classed at the head of the list. Its broad, sword-like foliage and 5 to 6 feet tall, branched spikes of large, fragrant, drooping, creamy-white flowers during June make it an effective plant for all positions.

Index

Spring Hill Nurseries

...the good will and integrity that we have maintained...
...bout sixty years of business.

...tors, nor do we wish to compare ourselves with the...
...and to give our customers the benefit derived from the reduction **made possible on this overhead expense item.**

LOCATED ON THE DAYTON & TROY TRACTION AND B. & O. RAILROAD, 14 MILES FROM DAYTON. A DIRECT LINE TO ANY PART OF THE COUNTRY.

REFERENCES:
ANY BANK
R. G. DUNN & CO.
BRADSTREET'S AGENCY

OVER 60 YEARS EXPERIENCE

LONG DISTANCE PHONE

Spring Hill Nurseries

Peter Bohlender & Sons

Tippecanoe City, Ohio, (Miami County)

Dear Friend:

Every bit of stock offered in our catalog is of the best quality possible to be grown and with each tree, shrub or vine that we sell, goes the good will and integrity that we have maintained throughout sixty years of business.

We have not one word of complaint to make about any of our competitors, nor do we wish to compare ourselves with any other firm. We know that we will furnish you the best quality of stock, guaranteed true to name, express prepaid on all orders of $4.00 or more, and to reach you in good first class condition. Can you ask any more?

We have always maintained our business on a cash basis, thereby enabling us to cut the expense of caring for running accounts and to give our customers the benefit derived from the reduction made posssible on this overhead expense item.

Our business, naturally, has prospered. We have made many steadfast business friends in the last sixty years, we want to make many more during our future years as nurserymen. We are trying to make each customer a friend. We are going to succeed in so doihg as we have done in the past.

We realize that our customers may sometimes desire a short time credit. We shall be glad to extend a ten days credit to responsible people. You may have your stock shipped and pay for it ten days after receipt by just stating on the order blank the number of acres you own, or improved city lot, and the county and state in which same is located. Thus we believe all may be benefitted and an elaborate credit system is thereby eliminated.

Trusting that you will favor us with your patronage and assuring you of our personal attention to each order, we are

Sincerely yours,

Spring Hill Nurseries
M.O. Dept. J.B. Crouch,

Bulbs For Spring Planting

Most of the bulbs for spring planting produce beautiful blossoms, but some of them are raised principally for the foliage effects. Altogether they are much to be desired, and no garden is complete without several dozen of these bulbs. They are all of easy culture and they will grow in most any good garden soil. Of course, like other plants, they will amply repay the caretaker for any extra work bestowed upon them. All of the bulbs that we are offering are first-class and will give good satisfaction. After the first killing frost in the autumn, all of these bulbs should be lifted, allowed to dry off, and then store in a dry place, secure from frost.

GLADIOLUS

CALADIUM (Elephant Ear)

ESCULENTUM—This is a splendid foliage plant that has proven very satisfactory and worthy of cultivation everywhere, as they add a tropical appearance to any lawn. To get the best results from Caladium bulbs, they should be planted in well-enriched soil and given plenty of water. The bulbs may be kept over winter by taking them up as soon as the leaves have been killed by frost; dry gradually in a cool, airy place; after dried, place in a shallow box with dry sand and keep them in a dry cellar where they will not freeze.

Mammoth size bulbs, 14 to 18 inches in circumference, 50c each.

No. 1X size bulbs, 11 to 14 inches in circumference, 35c each.

No. 1 size bulbs, 9 to 11 inches in circumference, 25c each.

DAHLIAS

One of the best late summer and autumn flowering plants and now enjoying a wide popularity. Our Dahlias are only sorted up in colors and not named varieties. We can furnish them in pink, red, yellow and white. Large size tubers, 6 for 50c.

GLADIOLIAS

A splendid old-fashioned flower. This has become a general favorite with everybody and very greatly prized wherever grown. The handsome shadings of these blossoms have no equal and are a delight to all. The bulbs we offer are the best assortment of mixed we have ever offered, made up of the kinds that sell at double the price we are offering here.

Mixed Bulbs, No. 1 size, 10 for 75c; 25 for $1.35; 100 for $5.00.

Can furnish long list of varieties, best assorted No. 1 Bulbs, 10 for $1.00; 25 for $1.75; 100 for $6.00.

CANNAS

The Cannas, with their large, various-colored leaves, easily hold second place for producing a tropical effect on the lawn. Excellent effects may be secured by planting them singly or by planting in small clumps in the hardy shrubbery border. Against a heavy background of green, the bright-colored, variously-marked leaves show to their best and are very attractive and interesting. Following kinds, 10c each; 10 for $1.00; $7.50 per 100 roots.

CANNAS (Continued)

BLACK PRINCE—Velvety maroon, green foliage; 3 to 4 feet.

GLADIATOR—Yellow spotted; green; 4 ft.

RICHARD WALLACE—Canary yellow, green foliage; 4½ feet.

AUSTRIA—Pure canary yellow; 3 feet.

WYOMING—Orange, foliage purple; 7 feet.

PENNSYLVANIA—Orange scarlet; green; 5 ft.

INDIANA—Golden orange; green foliage; 3-4 ft.

SHENANDOAH—Salmon, bronze foliage; 6 ft.

DAVID HARUM—Vermilion scarlet; bronze foliage; 3½ feet.

KING HUMBERT—Orange scarlet; foliage coppery bronze; 5 to 6 feet.

CHEROKEE—Dark red; foliage green; 4-5 ft.

AMERICA—Orange; foliage bronze; 6 to 7 ft.

LILIES AND OTHER BULBS

The Lilies have always been looked upon as among the noblest of the garden flowers. Their conspicuous and beautiful flowers and stately forms appeal strongly to the eye. Most varieties are very fragrant and are especially desirable for cut flowers. Lilies are 30c each.

JAPANESE LILIES

Beautiful, artistic Lilies of the following varieties:

RUBRUM—Handsome, dark, pinkish-red flowers. Extra strong growing sort.

ALBUM—Beautiful white, or nearly white flower.

SPECIOSUM—White, more or less tinted with pink and dotted with red.

Poor stock is expensive at any price; quality is what counts.

Serving the same customers for more than forty years is proof that we only offer what we know to be the best.

CANNAS

THE BENTON REVIEW SHOP, FOWLER, IND.
HORTICULTURAL PRINTERS

A Word About the American Association of Nurserymen's Trademark

The best agricultural and farm papers throughout the country heartily indorse the American Association of Nurserymen, and point to their trade mark as a guarantee to the purchaser of nursery stock, and a proof of the business integrity of those who are members of the Association. They say, "It is the right way." These men have looked into this matter thoroughly before making such a declaration. The Association has nothing to do with establishing of prices, but it is meant to be a protection to everyone buying nursery stock.

We are willing to extend credit to anyone desiring it, but we can not afford to do a credit business and add to the price or deduct from the quality of the goods to offset the loss from those who do not pay their bills, neither can you afford it.

Our Terms

Place your order with the Spring Hill Nurseries, and it will receive prompt and careful attention, and rest assured you will be supplied with stock true to name and of the very best quality.

Shipments

We will ship stock when wanted by our customers and when so directed, otherwise we forward stock at the proper time and in the best season for the stock, and the benefit of our patrons. The conditions of the weather have to be considered in this matter.

Peter Bohlender & Sons

Spring Hill Nurseries,   Tippecanoe City, Ohio

CPSIA information can be obtained
at www.ICGtesting.com
Printed in the USA
BVHW041057271218
536518BV00006B/201/P